CW01123786
A. MERRITT'S FANTASY
CELEBRATED CLASSICS OF FANTASY
25¢
APR.
MAGAZINE
FEATURING THE NINTH LIFE by JACK MANN
LONE ISLE
E. CHARLES VIVIAN
GHOST·CANYON
BARRY·LYND

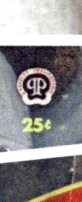

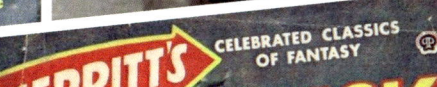

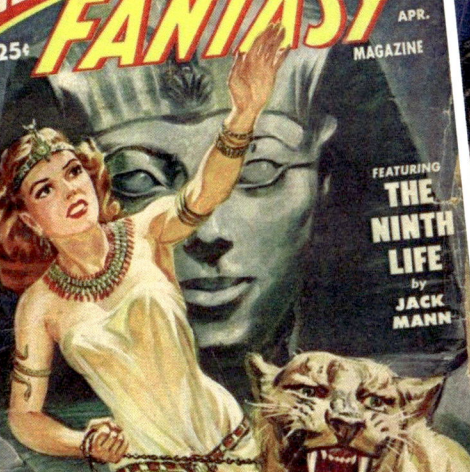

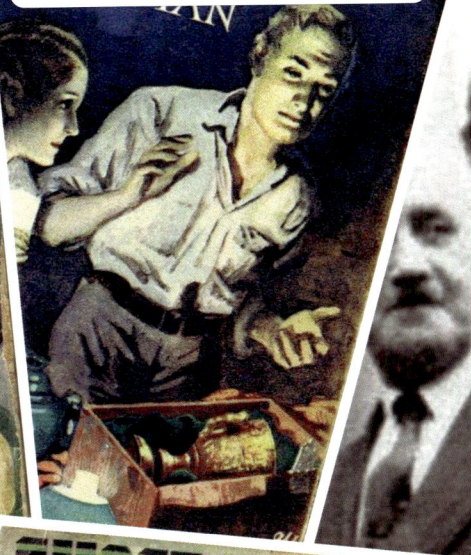

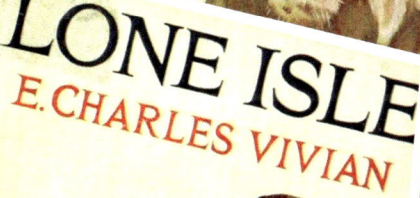

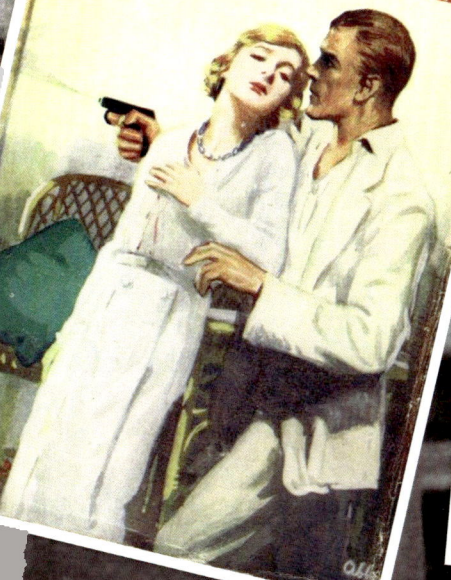

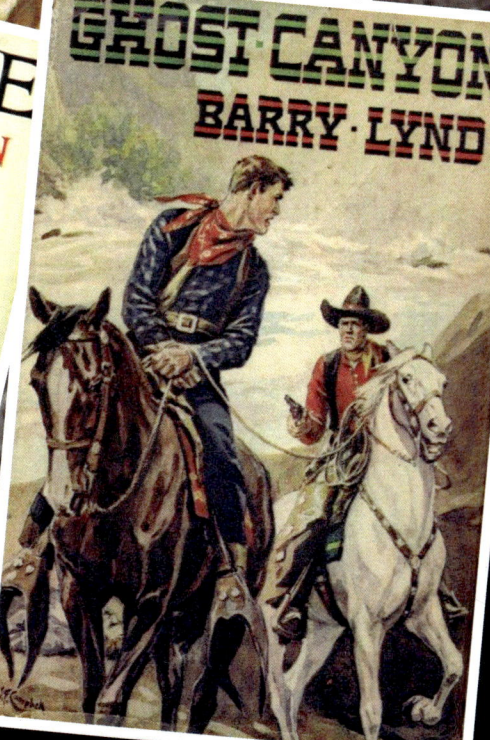

E Charles Vivian (1882–1947) was one of the most prolific popular writers of the 1920s and 1930s. Acclaimed for his fantasy and detective stories by fellow writers such as Dorothy L. Sayers and Eden Phillpotts, he also wrote under other pseudonyms. Only after his death was he revealed to be 'Jack Mann' whose supernatural detective series is still highly praised and reprinted.

After his death Vivian's work fell into obscurity and even the facts of his life were lost. This first biography has been a work of detection in itself as the writer managed to track down Vivian's real name and finally contact his daughter and family, discovering the reason why Vivian's estate did not promote his work after his death.

Vivian became editor of Hutchinson's *Adventure Story Magazine* and *Mystery Story Magazine*. He published ninety-five titles mainly as E. Charles Vivian, Jack Mann, even his own name Charles Cannell, and some dubious western novels as Barry Lynd.

The Shadow of Mr. Vivian

THE SHADOW OF MR. VIVIAN

The Life of E. Charles Vivian (1882-1947)

Peter Berresford Ellis

2014

THE SHADOW OF MR. VIVIAN
The Life of E. Charles Vivian (1882–1947)
Copyright © Peter Berresford Ellis 2014

Published in June 2014 by PS Publishing Ltd. by arrangement with the author. All rights reserved by the author. The right of Peter Berresford Ellis to be identified as Author of this Work has been asserted by him in accordance with the Copyright, Designs and Patents Act 1988.

First Edition

ISBN 978-1-848637-83-2

Design & Layout by Michael Smith

Printed and bound in England by T. J. International

PS PUBLISHING LTD
Grosvenor House
1 New Road
Hornsea, HU18 1PG
England

editor@pspublishing.co.uk
www.pspublishing.co.uk

Contents

Introduction vii
Chapter 1 – Family and Background 3
Chapter 2 – The Army Years .23
Chapter 3 – A Career in Journalism 40
Chapter 4 – Editorship 58
Chapter 5 – Adventure and Mystery 76
Chapter 6 – France 91
Chapter 7 – The Old Bailey Trial 106
Chapter 8 – Inspector Byrne and Others 121
Chapter 9 – 'Jack Mann' 128
Chapter 10 – Inspector Head of Westingborough . . .140
Chapter 11 – The Last Years 153
Bibliography 171
Acknowledgements 177

INTRODUCTION

E. Charles Vivian was not only a prolific and popular author of the 1920s and 1930s, with ninety-four titles published under his own name and his three pseudonyms, together with short stories, articles and serials, in which he employed other pen-names, but he was also a highly respected and influential editor of some of Britain's leading popular fiction magazines of his day. He created *Hutchinson's Adventure–Story Magazine* and *Mystery–Story Magazine*, and was their editor for the first years of their life. Both magazines take their place in the Valhalla of popular literature.[1]

The author and critic, Mike Ashley, wrote in his *Who's Who in Horror and Fantasy Fiction* (1977): 'It is strange that a writer as popular as Evelyn Charles Vivian was in the 1920s and 1930s should now be unknown and details of his life lost in obscurity...'[2]

Today Vivian is, indeed, all but forgotten. Even Katharine Vivian Ashton, Vivian's daughter, commented on recent years: 'I never met anyone who has heard of him'.[3] Only a small group of aficionados of weird fiction and detective mysteries remember and read his work. The last time that some of his titles were in print in the United Kingdom was back in the early 1950s, although he has fared slightly better in the USA where several titles were reprinted in the 1970s and 1980s. More recently, Vivian and Jack Mann titles became available from a number of small publishers in the USA in the belief the books were already out of copyright or that Vivian had no heirs and his estate did not exist. Vivian's granddaughter, Tess Blondel, had no idea that his work was still being reprinted.

Vivian's work was praised by critics as diverse as Dorothy L. Sayers, Eden Phillpotts, the American humorist and critic, Will Cuppy, and the renowned 'Torquemada' of the *London Observer*. As an editor, Vivian's memory has rated a passing mention in a few autobiographies by writers and journalists. It becomes clear that he was highly regarded in his field and, as an editor, influential on his generation of popular fiction writers. The present writer bought his first second-hand Vivian after the crime writer, Nicholas Blake (1904–1972), mentioned that he had devoured 'Inspector Head' novels as a young man and been very impressed by them.[4]

Yet Vivian remains essentially a man of mystery. Vivian was not even his real name. Eighteen-year-old Charles Henry Cannell ran away from home to join the army, adopting the name Evelyn Henry Vivian in 1900. This was later amended to Evelyn Charles Vivian which then, more or less, served him for the rest of his life. The mysteries of his life have been compounded by the fact that his London home was bombed during 1941, a few years before his death, and all his personal papers, diaries and letters were destroyed.[5] At the same time, the offices of his literary agent, John Farquharson, were bombed and his records of dealings with Vivian were obliterated. German bombs, too, destroyed the offices of his main publishers, Ward Lock & Co and Wright and Brown, in the famous incendiary raid on the City of London in December, 1940, destroying not only all file copies but volumes of correspondence and personal materials relating to their authors.

Vivian's only daughter, Katharine, who died in 2010, told me she had little knowledge of her father's origins, of his early adventurous life in South Africa and India, nor of his subsequent career in London journalism. Even during the period when she was growing up, when Vivian was at his most productive, most of the time she spent away at boarding school in Kent and later at university in France. At that time she believed she had a close relationship with her father. She recalled that they often had long discussions on writing and particularly poetry, which was a mutually favourite subject. Many enthusiastic bibliographers of Vivian's works believed there could be only one Charles Vivian writing for the popular magazines at this time. They therefore ascribed to E. Charles Vivian scores of verse published by 'Charles Vivian' at the time. His daughter, Kitty Vivian was certain that her father did not write them.[6] She was also unaware of many of the writing pseudonyms which her father adopted during his prolific career. This story could merely serve to illustrate the way Vivian seemed to guard the details of his personal life, even from his immediate family. But there is another reason.

It was when I met Katharine's daughter, Tess Blondel, that I realised there was another problem why Katharine was so reticent about revealing too much of her father's personal life. He had a mistress who made claims on him during the 1920s and 1930s, which finally resulted in a blackmail case and a court decision that did not rebound well on Vivian. It resulted in the judge stating that Vivian was untruthful and forwarding the papers to Public Prosecutor's Office, at which point Vivian took himself off on a Mediterranean cruise.

Katharine was always reticent when it came to personal details and, in retrospect, I came to the conclusion that, perhaps out of an understandable loyalty to her mother, she wanted to protect her father's public figure and avoid delving too deeply into his private life. All these factors hindered my researches so that only little glimpses of light can now be cast on the shadow of his curious personality.

Another problem has been that all of Vivian's contemporaries, his friends and colleagues such as Norman Douglas, J. D. Beresford, Eden Phillpotts, Sheila Kaye-Smith, Harry Stephen Keeler, his agent John Farquharson and others, are now all dead and their papers dispersed or destroyed. Even in Edward Liveing's history of Ward Lock, the publishers of forty-three of his novels between 1927 and 1942, he does not even rate a passing mention. Neither does his name appear in most of the biographies of those he worked for and with—for example, Ford Madox Ford, W. T. Stead and Hilaire Belloc. There is, curiously, not even a passing mention of him in

J. D. Beresford's autobiography, nor in *Leaves of Memory*, the autobiographical sketch of his friend and fellow Ward Lock writer Archibald Thomas Pechey, better known under the pseudonyms 'Valentine' and Mark Cross.

Documentation on his life is sparse to say the least. Neither did Vivian appear to be a man who courted publicity apart from reviews of his works. There appear to be no interviews with him in literary journals, other publications, or even discussions on his life and work. When he died there were only a few lines of obituary in the *Daily Telegraph* which simply mentioned the fact of his authorship.[7] The lack of information about Vivian led the editor of *A. Merritt's Fantasy Magazine* in New York, when republishing a 'Jack Mann' story in April 1950, to print an appeal for information about the then whereabouts of the mysterious author, not realising that he had then been dead for three years:

'Pen names are never unusual, so you will not be surprised to learn that 'Jack Mann' is none other than that very famous author of fantasy, Evelyn Charles Vivian. Amongst his best-known works are *City of Wonder* and *Maker of Shadows*. And speaking of shadows... here is a job for all you fantasy enthusiasts: what has become of Mr Vivian? He's an Englishman who, during the last war, lived in Chelsea, London. But since 1947 we have been unable to trace him!'[8]

It was on October 22, 1976 that the American publisher, Donald M. Grant, wrote to me asking if I knew any details of Vivian's life story. I knew as much as any other reader who had enjoyed some of his weird tales and his Inspector Head mysteries—which was virtually nothing. The idea of researching Vivian's life was pushed to the back of my mind for well over a decade while I worked on other projects. Then in February 1990, I managed to trace and make contact with Vivian's only daughter, Mrs Katharine Ashton. I fondly imagined that the research project would become an easy task as a result of this contact; but five years later E. Charles Vivian remained an enigmatic personality. He was truly 'a maker of shadows'.

He is, however, deserving of a niche in the 'Valhalla of English Letters' not only because of his role as the influential editor of such

INTRODUCTION

genre fiction magazines as the *Adventure-Story Magazine*, and *Mystery-Story Magazine*, but for his own literary contribution. In two particular areas, I would argue, he is out-standing with his 'weird tales', including the 'lost race fantasies', and with his 'Inspector Head' detective mysteries.

To aficionados of detective mysteries, Vivian's 'Inspector Head' novels, written mainly during the 1930s, remain splendidly crafted works which can stand alongside any similar genre tales of the period and, indeed, appear better than many whose popularity have survived today. They were highly regarded at the time. Dorothy L. Sayers, creator of 'Lord Peter Wimsey', confessed to being a fan of Vivian's rural detective.[9] In 1936, while editing detective stories for the London *Evening Standard*, she invited Vivian to write an 'Inspector Head' tale especially for the series.[10] Vivian's Home Counties background to the 'Inspector Head' novels is drawn with the careful eye of an artist which causes some of these novels to transcend the average mystery story. The sleepy town of Westingborough and its surrounding district becomes a very real place. *Seventeen Cards* (1935) is an outstanding example of his 'Inspector Head' *ouvrage*, which was the novel that first caught Dorothy L. Sayers' critical eye.

Vivian had, earlier in his career, written several adventure fantasies, mainly of the 'lost race' variety in the H. Rider Haggard mould, which had established his name in the realms popular fiction. Had he written nothing else but *Fields of Sleep* (1923), he would have been assured of a mention in any survey of fantasy writing. Michael Joseph, soon to establish his own publishing house and then a young critic on *The Smart Set*, hailed it as 'one of the greatest works of modern imaginative fiction.'[11] Like Rider Haggard, Vivian was able to produce remarkable adventure tales of the discovery of lost lands and exotic peoples, still highly prized by enthusiasts of that form of literature today.

But the books which have kept Vivian's name 'green', particularly in the United States where they were reprinted through the 1960s–1980s, were a series of occult mysteries written under the pseudonym Jack Mann. They featured a detective called 'Gees' (Gregory George

xi

Gordon Green). The remarkably scarce first editions of these books now fetch £250 and more from avid collectors of the genre. Jack Mann has received more than a passing genuflection in studies of fantasy literature.

If one were to look for a reason as to why Vivian's work is now generally forgotten, it might be argued that Vivian could never be classed as a 'bestseller' in the same way his literary rivals Rider Haggard and Edgar Wallace were. His works sold well, sometimes certain titles sold very well indeed. During the 1920s and 1930s his Ward Lock titles were issued in an average of two, three and sometimes four different editions. Moreover, they were well received by critics and he had a large library following. Therefore, his readership was far in excess of his sales. But being popular while one is alive is not a guarantee of remembrance after death. Nor is it an assurance of a lasting place in the Literary Valhalla. Indeed, Vivian's contemporary, Talbot Mundy (1879–1940) was one of the highest paid writers of adult adventure fiction of the period. His books sold in their tens of thousands on both sides of the Atlantic and in translation. His output was 46 novels, two short story collections and two omnibus collections. Several novels were made into films, one of them by the formidable John Ford. His work proliferated in the popular fiction magazines of the day. Critics ranked him with Rider Haggard and Rudyard Kipling. Yet in the 1970s, just thirty years after the death of Talbot Mundy, his British publishers Hutchinson, who had made a tidy fortune out of Mundy's work, could blandly confess that they had never heard of him![12]

What hope, then, of a more modest and less flamboyant writer like Vivian, whose work had never made it to the silver screen, being remembered?

But, it can be argued, some writers are remembered as 'great writers' when their sales scarcely make the printing of their work a viable commercial proposition. John Sutherland, in his study *Bestsellers*, has pointed out the curious phenomenon that Literature (with a capital 'L') is often little read and reaches minimal sales yet receives great accolades from literary critics, who have conventionally paid little attention to more popular authors. Through sheer repetition in Press and Media and critical works, these writers become household names but few people ever go so far as to read their works.[13]

Vivian clearly wished to be regarded as a serious novelist. His early works certainly fall into this class. He showed 'considerable promise', that most terrible critical back-handed commendation which is really a form of literary dismissal. Perhaps he could have eventually persuaded critics that he had more than 'promise'. But Vivian was a writer who also had to live and he had a flare for fine, exciting story telling. By 1923, therefore, Vivian had become identified in the minds of his readers with popular fiction. Yet he continued to write 'serious fiction', resorting to the use of his real name, Charles Cannell, as a pen-name when his publishers thought his novels would not be taken seriously by those who had come to associate the name Vivian with fantasy.

In the 1940s he made a final attempt to write 'serious fiction' using the name Vivian, and was immediately castigated by the *Times Literary Supplement* for 'pushing Inspector Head out of his pages', implying that Vivian's readers now expected a proper detective mystery when they saw his name.[14] This drew a very untypical response from the publicity shy Vivian, who wrote a sharp retort to the *Times Literary Supplement*, pointing out: 'It is distinctly stated on the jacket that this is a "novel", which is different from a mystery story...'[15]

There is, perhaps, another argument why his work is ignored by most modern literary historians and critics, and that is in the very diversity of his prolific output. During the 1930s, for example, he was producing sometimes five and six novels a year, among which was a motley output ranging from detective fiction under Vivian, some serious work as Charles Cannell, his weird fiction as Jack Mann, and even some poor quality westerns as Barry Lynd. The quality of these works was somewhat varied. Critics have a tendency to be slighting to prolific writers of varied quality, and the good work tends to be ignored or dismissed in the same contemptuous manner as the bad. Even Talbot Mundy's more moderate output was once dismissed by a jaundiced *Times Literary Supplement* critic who commented: 'Novels stream from his industrious pen. This perhaps is a pity. Mr Mundy would possibly do better work if he did a little less work.'[16]

Vivian was twice as prolific as Mundy but, unlike Mundy, he did not keep to one particular genre. While he wanted to be regarded as a 'serious novelist' he was, at the same time, achieving a reputation as a genre writer but not just in one genre. That prolific diversity has caused some, glancing over his work, to conclude that he was a 'grub-street writer', a 'penny-a-liner', turning out material for whoever paid him. Perhaps if Vivian had kept rigidly to one or other genre he might well have been more locked in the public memory for that particular area of writing. For example, his 'serious fiction' was often set in East Anglia, utilising his own childhood background, and demonstrated that he had a fine ear for the dialect of his native Norfolk. Had he stuck to the production of the series of serious novels set in Norfolk he might have been identified as a 'county-writer', as Hardy was to Wessex or Sheila Kaye-Smith, who was a friend of Vivian, was to Sussex; or, indeed, as his other good friend, Eden Phillpotts, was sometimes regarded to Devonshire.[17]

Had Vivian concentrated on boys' adventure fiction, for he had become a popular contributor to *Boys' Own Paper* as early as 1913, he might have received more than a passing genuflection in *The Men Behind Boys' Fiction* (1970).[18] In fact, little of his boys' fiction was collected in book form. Only four juvenile titles were ever published, leaving many short stories and serials consigned to oblivion in the pages of *Boys' Own Paper*.

Had he kept faithfully to detective mysteries his work may have outlived the 1930s and 1940s, as that of other mystery writers of the period have done. It was certainly as good as, and better than, the work which has had a nostalgic rebirth in recent years. Had he concentrated on adventure fantasy or weird fantasy, his name might have tripped as readily off the tongue as Rider Haggard.

The argument which I am making could be reinforced by pointing out that he is now better known in the United States today than in his native country as a fantasy adventure writer, because the American publishers were more selective with what they published by Vivian. Although he was first published in the US in 1910, US publishers took only two of his 'serious novels', developing him as a writer of fantasy adventure whereby prestigious magazines such as *Argosy, Golden Fleece, Famous Fantastic Mysteries* and *Merritt's Fantasy Magazine* serialised his fiction. In all, only seventeen of Vivian's 94 titles were published in American editions during his lifetime.

To simply dismiss Vivian as a talented 'hack', churning out work for whoever paid him, is to do him an injustice. Certainly he was a professional writer. His interests, however, were eclectic. He was what could be called a 'Renaissance Man' with his hand in many departments of the craft of writing. He was a compulsive writer but, above all, he was a man with a living to make and a wife and child to keep, for he had inherited a sense of insecurity from his wastrel of a father. It could be argued that it was his insecure childhood, his father's constant business failures and general financial irresponsibility that made Vivian more conscious of providing a stable home and security for his own family. Conflict between sons and fathers became an almost constant theme of his fiction. I would argue that his novel *Ash* (1925) was a major piece of self-analysis, a therapeutic autobiographical study, in which Vivian attempted to lay the ghosts of his unhappy childhood to rest.

As a writer his output is awe-inspiring; from studies on the British Army, cited as an authority as recently as 1991 in *The British Military Dilemma in Ireland*,[19] to a standard guide book on Peru; from sheer journalese works such as a study on the Red Cross and a history of aeronautics, to juvenile fiction such as his tremendously popular bestseller retelling of the adventures of *Robin Hood*, first published in 1927 and still being regularly reprinted by the same publisher twenty-three years later; from serious 'literary' novels, one reputedly banned by London magistrates in 1912, the stock of which had to be ceremoniously burnt by his publisher Heinemann.[20] From fantasy adventures to detective mysteries; from occult thrillers to westerns. E. Charles Vivian produced them all. In all that prodigious work there is a great deal one can discard as being of 'pot-boiler' standard. But there is also much that warrants our attention. Certain of his novels are still worthy of a continuing public readership, rather than being consigned to an occasional dissection by literary morticians.

Even if Vivian's own literary contributions are not sufficient to secure him that place in the Literary Valhalla, then his own work as an editor should surely do so. From editorial assistant on Ford Madox Ford's famous *English Review*, to assistant editor on W. T. Stead's *Review of Reviews* and then to assistant editor of the weekly *Land and Water*, Vivian proceeded to the editorship of the weekly magazine *Flying* (1917–1919). Then in 1922 he was asked by the publisher Walter Hutchinson to join his company to originate, develop and launch what were to prove two of Hutchinson's most successful popular fiction monthlies—*Adventure-Story* (1922) and *Mystery-Story* (1923). Vivian's two magazines, for they were as much his creation as they were part of the Hutchinson magazine empire, attracted some of the greatest names in popular fiction of the day— from Rider Haggard to Edgar Wallace, from Rafael Sabatini to Sax Rohmer, from Johnston McCulley (creator of *Zorro*), to 'Sapper', H. Bedford-Jones and Arthur O. Friel.

This study can be no more than an argument for the right of E. Charles Vivian to that niche in the Literary Valhalla. His work is certainly freely available to critical scrutiny, but the facts of his life, in spite of years of research, are scanty. He remains a man of mystery. One can only hazard at some of his motivations and the reasons behind certain events in his early life and those in his later life, which were sadly compounded by reticence of his daughter. The Vivian of flesh and blood only emerges into the light now and then. He seems to pass through life mainly as a shadow.

But such study of the facts of biography as I know them would, I suggest, make the following deduction possible: that Vivian courted mystery in his life because of an unhappy childhood; a bad relationship with his father which reached a triggering point at the time of his eighteenth birthday in October, 1900, which caused him, a few weeks later, to present himself to the army recruiting sergeant at Colchester, giving not only a false name but, for his next of kin, the name and address of a ten year old girl who bore no legal or blood relationship to him. Try as one might, the mystery of why he gave the name of that girl has been impossible to entirely resolve. In it, I believe, lies the answer to his subsequent reticence about revealing any details of his personal life. The character of his father, and Vivian's conflict with him, was coupled with a sense of humiliation about his background. His eldest sister, displaying her social pretensions, had elevated her father when declaring his occupation at her marriage to the rank of 'gentleman', when he was, at the time, a farm labourer. Vivian himself told his daughter that his father was a 'gentleman farmer'. But while Vivian's father, the son of a working farmer, had once rented a farm for a few years mainly on money borrowed from his wife, he had spent most of his life simply as a farm labourer.

We can make some informed speculations, based on the facts we know, about the reasons for the scene in the Colchester Army Recruiting Office on November 15 1900, when an unhappy young man giving his name as 'Evelyn Henry Vivian' appeared before the recruiting sergeant. We can speculate, but many mysteries remain. These constitute the Gordian knot of any prospective biographical study of Vivian. Alas, although the knot has been loosened a little—indeed, the knot itself has only been revealed by the current research, for even Vivian's daughter knew nothing of it—it is still tied fast, protecting all but 'The Shadow of Mr Vivian' from public scrutiny.[21]

Notes

[1.] These magazines were launched in 1922 and 1923 and were Vivian's own creation.
[2.] *Who's Who in Horror and Fantasy Fiction*, Mike Ashley, Hamish Hamilton, London, 1977, p. 176.
[3.] Katharine Vivian Ashton to author, letter, August 28, 1991.
[4.] This conversation took place in the mid-1960s at a party at William Collins' offices in St James. Nicholas Blake was, of course, the poet-laureate, Cecil

Day-Lewis, who used the pseudonym to write a number of original and successful detective novels. Sadly he does not mention Vivian in his autobiography *Buried Day* (1960).
5. Katharine Ashton to author, letter, March 22, 1990.
6. Katharine Ashton to author, letter, October 13, 1993.
7. *The Daily Telegraph*, May 23, 1947
8. *Merritt's Fantasy Magazine*, April, 1950.
9. *Sunday Times*, February 17, 1935
10. *Evening Standard*, August 31, 1936. The story 'Locked In' was reprinted in *My Best Mystery Story*, Faber and Faber, London, 1939.
11. *The Smart Set*, October, 1923.
12. 'Writer Forgotten?' by Peter Berresford Ellis, *The Author*, Spring, 1992. See also: *The Last Adventurer; The Life of Talbot Mundy* by Peter Berresford Ellis, Donald M. Grant Inc, Rhode Island, US, 1984.
13. *Bestseller*, John Sutherland, Routledge & Kegan Paul, London, 1981.
14. *Times Literary Supplement*, May 23, 1942.
15. *Times Literary Supplement*, June 6, 1942.
16. *Times Literary Supplement*, February 26, 1931.
17. It could, of course, be argued that Phillpotts, when he died at the age of 98, had published over 250 novels in many different genres, which makes Vivian's output seem meagre. But, then, Eden Phillpotts himself now seems in danger of neglect. There is not even an entry on him in the current edition of *The Reader's Encyclopædia* (3rd ed., 1988).
18. *The Men Behind Boys Fiction*, W. O. G. Lofts and Derek Adley, Howard Baker, London, 1970.
19. *The British Military Dilemma in Ireland*, Elizabeth A. Muenger, University Press of Kansas, Lawrence, Kansas, USA, 1991. p. 55, 104, 240.
20. *William Heinemann*, John St. John, Heinemann, London, 1990, p. 46/47.
21. 'The Shadow of E. Charles Vivian' was the title of an article by the current author and Richard Dalby in *The Book and Magazine Collector*, May, 1997 (issue No.158).

THE SHADOW OF MR.VIVIAN

CHAPTER ONE

FAMILY AND BACKGROUND

If the old folkloric verse about birthdays carries any weight and 'Saturday's child works for its living' then E. Charles Vivian became a typical 'Saturday's child'; that is, if his prodigious writing output is placed on the scales.

Vivian was born Charles Henry Cannell on Saturday, October 21, 1882, at Forster's Farm, just outside the village of Bedingham in Norfolk. His father, James Henry Cannell, had been running the farm for three years as a tenant farmer. By coincidence, Forster's Farm was scarcely a mile from the Ditchingham estate of Sir Henry Rider Haggard, which Haggard had acquired by marriage to Louisa Margitson, the only child of Major John Margitson (d. 1868), a prominent Norfolk landowner. At the time of Charles Henry Cannell's birth, Rider Haggard and his wife Louise had recently returned from farming in South Africa. Haggard had just published his first book *Cetywayo and his White Neighbours*. It appeared in June, 1882, a few months before Charles Henry was born. Haggard, in fact, also farmed 104 acres in Bedingham at Moat Farm which bordered the property of Charles Henry's grandfather, John Cannell.[1]

The village of Bedingham, five miles north-west from Bungay and eleven miles south from Norwich, has an ancient history with Roman remains found in the vicinity. Its records date from the Domesday Book but, as a village, its birth was clearly in an early settlement of

Angles, being the 'Ham of Bedda's people'. Its population, in the year Charles Henry was born, was 293 persons. In *A Farmer's Year* (1899) Haggard spoke of Bedingham as being 'scarcely changed' since the time of William the Conqueror. There had been a priory there in 1318, standing close to the village church of St Andrews until the Reformation. The parish registers date from 1555.

Haggard, in his book on farming, dwells much on his farm at Bedingham.[2] It is a pity that he mentions nothing of James Henry Cannell of Forster's Farm, nor his father, John Cannell, who owned and farmed Willow Farm. But then he was not to realise that James' only son Charles Henry would one day change his name to E. Charles Vivian and make a reputation for himself in the same genre of literature as Haggard himself.

Perhaps it was not merely a coincidence that the paths of these men were to cross when Vivian, in 1922, joined Hutchinson as an editor at exactly the same time that Haggard was persuaded to leave his publishers, Cassell's, and join Hutchinson's stable of authors. However, a few of Haggard's books had been serialised in Hutchinson magazines before this date, but he had never been published in book form by Hutchinson before Vivian joined the firm.

The Cannell family had been in East Anglia since the turn of the nineteenth century. The family had originated in the Isle of Man (Ellan Vannin). The name is one of the most ancient and popular Manx names from the Manx *Mac Dhomhnaill* (from the ancient Celtic *Dumnovalos*—'world mighty'). Anglicisation of the phonetics had produced the form 'Cannell'. An ancestor of the Cannells, Hugh Cannell, vicar of Kirk Malew (c.1585–1670) is noted as being the first to teach the Scriptures in Manx when Latin was dropped by the Anglican Church in favour of the vernacular usage. Hugh Cannell assisted Bishop John Phillips in translating the *Book of Common Prayer* into Manx (1610) as well as the *Bible*.[3] While the *Book of Common Prayer* survived, there has been no discovery of a manuscript of the translation of the *Bible*.

Three Cannell brothers arrived from the island at Great Yarmouth in the early years of the nineteenth century. They were fishermen.[4]

These Manxmen were James, born in 1783, and twins John and Charles, born on September 7, 1784. The reason for their move from their still predominantly Gaelic-speaking island to Great Yarmouth was the deterioration of economic conditions on the island. In May 1765, by purchase, George III of England had become sovereign of the island. The island had thereby become a dependency of the British Crown. While the Tynwald, the Manx parliament, the oldest continuous national parliament in the world, continued to meet and legislate for the islanders, the Manx had effectively become ruled by the English Home office, who appointed a series of Governors and Lt. Governors. The island went through a period of strict financial control from London, which brought about the decay of farming, fishing and the island's rich trading links, with an alarming rise of unemployment. It was these strictures on the fishing industry that induced the three young Cannell brothers to take their ships and seek out a new port. Frank Cannell says that the brothers wanted to be nearer to the rich North Sea fishing grounds to which, while operating from the island, they had previously been prohibited.[5]

The Cannell brothers brought with them their strict Methodism which was to be a point of contention in young Charles Henry's youth. The island had been converted by John Wesley (1703–1791) himself, making two tours in 1777 and 1780. He toured the island with an interpreter, and while he was no friend to the Manx language ('we should do everything in our power to abolish it from the earth, and persuade every member of our Society to learn and talk English')[6] his acolytes had to use the language as the only medium by which to convert the island. By 1800 some 10% of islanders were vehement Methodists and this figure was to grow. One Cannell descendant recalled that the Cannell brothers' library contained copies of *Rulyn yn Pobble Enmyssit Methodistyn* (Rules of the People Called Methodists), published by J. Nuttall of Liverpool in 1800, and Reverend Thomas Christian's translation of Milton's *Paradise Lost* (*Phargys Callyt*) published by Briscoe's of Douglas in 1796. Thus, the progenitors of the East Anglian Cannells were Manx speaking when they arrived in Great Yarmouth. Mrs Joyce Bond, a

Cannell descendant, also confirms that 'The Cannells lived in Bedingham for most of the last century, but they didn't make use of the church—they were very strict Methodists.'[7]

One of the twins, John Cannell (1784–1879), had a son Charles. By 1858 Charles had become established as a merchant in Great Yarmouth. In that year he bought Willow Farm, near the priory, at Bedingham. It encompassed 90 acres. He rented it to a John Thain during the following year. In 1870 Charles' younger brother John (1815–1894), also a trader in Yarmouth, bought the farm from his brother. It is recorded in the Manor Court Books that John Cannell not only owned the farm but was living on it and working it. John, at the late age of fifty-five years, threw himself enthusiastically into farming and became moderately successful. With his wife Eliza, three years his junior, he also produced a family of ten children whose descendants still live within the area.

The historian Christopher Hibbert sums up the condition of farmers during this period in these words:

'Most of these holdings were rented from local landowners with whom the farmers might mix in the hunting field or at the cattle show but from whom they were separated by as wide a social gulf as separated the prosperous solicitor from his ill-paid clerk. The larger farmer, living in a comfortable house with servants inside and labourers in the fields outside, was a man of some consequence; but he had no pretensions to being a gentleman. He did not take much interest in local affairs; he usually steered clear of the parson; and had little use for education. The smaller farmer was obliged to work a great deal harder, finding it as much as he could do to look after his land and animals with the help of his family and perhaps one or two hired labourers.'[8]

John Cannell certainly fell into the latter class.

John's eldest son was James Henry Cannell born in 1849. James Henry had two elder sisters, Maryann, born 1845 and Elizabeth, born 1848. The next child after James Henry was John George, born in 1850. More children were to follow: Eliza, born 1851; Charles in 1853; Ambrose in 1856; Carlos in 1858 and Frederick in 1859; and

Jabez in 1862.[9] All his children were born before John went into the farming business.

As well as utilising his children as farmhands as they grew up, John also employed two labourers and a maid. John Cannell was a working farmer, a plain, blunt man with strict Nonconformist views that you were not entitled to that for which you did not work.

His eldest son, James Henry was twenty-one when his father took up farming. He had initially been employed in his father's fishmongery business in Yarmouth. Now he took up farm labouring with the prospect of taking over his father's 90 acre farm. He not only helped on his father's farm but hired himself out as a farm labourer to adjacent farmers. He was therefore able to rent his own cottage in Cock Street, in Bedingham. In 1879 he met an attractive, thirty-four year old widow, Louisa Anne Whisker. She was a Norfolk farmer's daughter. They were soon married.

Louisa had been born in Mattishall, Norfolk, the eldest child of Charles and Rosamund Tooley who farmed at Greengate. She had married a farmer named William Legood Whisker, one year her senior, on September 10, 1868. The marriage had taken place at the parish church at Hempnall. Louisa and William had no children and in 1876 William, then aged only 32 years, died suddenly. But in his will he left Louisa with the then substantial sum of £800.[10] It seems that William, on his mother's side, had a connection with Bedingham in the person of a cousin, George Legood, the village blacksmith. It might well have been during a visit to George Legood's family that Louisa first met James Henry Cannell.

The marriage of James Henry Cannell and Louisa Whisker took place at Bedingham parish church on December 2, 1879. The ceremony was carried out by the vicar, Reverend Frederick Charles Toole Hobbins, who had held the living since 1871. James Henry's younger brother Carlos, and his sister Eliza, stood as witnesses. James Henry decided that Cock Street was not the right location in which to start married life and he rented Forster's Farm with its 104 acres. He employed two labourers.[11] It is a Cannell family tradition that James Henry established himself as a tenant farmer utilising the £800 that Louisa bought into the marriage. This fits in well with the picture that Vivian subsequently painted of his father.[12]

Forster's Farm, curiously enough, has another tenuous link with Rider Haggard. The Forster family, who owned Forster's Farm, had also been owners of Moat Farm, which, in 1838 they had sold to the Margitsons in part exchange for Stag Farm, Bedingham. It was thus that Rider Haggard inherited Moat Farm.

If the conditions of Haggard's farm at Bedingham, described in *A Farmer's Year*, are to be judged as applying to James Henry's farm, then Forster's Farm was a difficult one to work:

'The Moat Farm at Bedingham is a heavy-land farm, in fact it would be difficult to find a heavier. Walk over it in wet weather, and five minutes of hard work will scarcely clean your boots, so "loving" is the country; walk over it in dry before the frost has broken up the clods in winter, or rain has slaked them in summer, and you must be careful lest you twist your ankle. But heavy land, unless it be very "thin in the skin", does not necessarily mean bad land. Indeed, if I were given the choice, would more lightly undertake a heavy-land farm in good order than one liable to "scald" which refuses to produce a crop of hay or roots unless deluged day by day with rain. Perhaps, however, this conviction owes something to the three years of drought which we have just experienced. The clay of Bedingham laughs at drought; as an old fellow there said to me, "It didn't never take no harm from it since Adam" and on it during these dry years I have grown some good barleys. For example, my Bedingham barley of 1896 fetched the highest price of any produced in this district that year.'[13]

But James Henry did not apparently share Haggard's enthusiasm for Bedingham farming. He did not make a success of his tenancy and sought to blame his failure on all manner of people other than himself. The Cannells recall that James Henry's indolent and complaining attitude brought him into conflict with his father John.[14] However, in fairness to James Henry, it should be pointed out that he started his farming venture in 1879, which was the worst and wettest summer that most farmers could remember and this was accompanied by an outbreak of liver-rot in sheep, which bankrupted many a farmer relying on sheep herds. In 1883 there was also a violent outbreak of foot-and-mouth disease. The price of English wheat and grain plummeted during this period as traders imported vast amounts of prairie-wheat and half of the country's grain supplies were bought from imports. In the wake of this, imports of frozen wheat began, of butter from Holland and even of live cattle. Farmers went bankrupt during this period in their scores; some one hundred thousand farm labourers left the land as wages fell sharply. Over a million members of the rural population emigrated.[15] Better and richer men than James Henry were not able to survive.

James Henry now had a growing family to support. The first child, a daughter, was born on February 18, 1881, and named Elizabeth Rosamond Eliza. In 1882 Charles Henry was born and on July 13, 1886, their last child Olive Louise was born. By this time James Henry's wife Louisa was forty-one years old. Her three children had been born late in life and she had become ill. It appeared that she needed rest and medical treatment. It was decided to send the eldest child, Elizabeth Rosamond, to Louisa's parents, Grandpa and Grandma Tooley, in Mattishall, to be looked after until Louisa had recovered her strength.[16] Such an arrangement was not uncommon in those days of the extended family.

By this time, young Charles Henry had started school at the local mixed parochial school, built by public subscription in 1863, and run with an iron rod by Miss Susan Baker, the village schoolmistress. It catered for children of the surrounding areas as well as Bedingham. Attendance, when Charles Henry commenced his schooling, averaged seventy pupils.

James Henry had mismanaged his financial affairs and this, coupled with the economic disaster that had hit farming generally in England, meant that he could not afford to keep the tenancy of Forster's Farm. His expectations of help from his father to resolve matters had not materialised. James Henry's father considered that the £800 Louisa had brought into her marriage (a wife's money became the property of her husband in those days) had been enough for his eldest son. John Cannell doubtless had his own economic problems in running his farm and he had nine other children to support and provide inheritances for. James Henry's brothers did not share their elder sibling's indolent attitudes. They had each rented farms of their own and, in spite of the economic climate, seemed to fare far better than their elder brother. It was Carlos who inherited John Cannell's Willow Farm when he died in 1894. The general family consensus seems to be that James Henry had tried to reach 'above his station' and was not prepared to put in the hard work necessary to make the farm profitable. This also seems to agree with the erroneous ideas passed down in James Henry's own family picturing him as a 'gentleman farmer'. When his daughter Elizabeth Rosamond married, at a time when James Henry had returned to being a farm labourer, she claimed his rank as 'gentleman'. The only resident 'gentleman farmer' in Bedingham at the time when James Henry was farming was, in fact, Major Clement W. J. Unthank of Intwood Hall, the principal landowner and local squire.

In 1925, under his own name Charles Cannell, Vivian published a novel entitled *Ash*. It is demonstrably autobiographical. The Cannell family still recall it as telling the story of the children of James Henry.[17] Indeed, James Henry was still alive at the time of its publication and in touch with a nephew who had also been called James Henry after him, and this was doubtless the source of confirmation of the information. The Cannell family appear in the novel as the 'Alston' family. Elizabeth is called 'Beth', while Charles Henry becomes 'Clifford' and his youngest sister Olive is 'Iris'. Vivian obviously had some key for these pseudonyms. 'Beth' was merely the diminutive of Elizabeth. For his maternal grandparents, Charles and Rosamund Tooley, he gave the name Street. At the time he was writing the book he was commuting into London Bridge Station which opens onto *Tooley Street*. Once the 'code' is known, the names are understandable. It is an intriguing piece of speculation to wonder if Charles Henry subsequently saw the play 'Where the Rainbow Ends' in 1911. It was written by Clifford Mills, and its central character was a Rosamund. It was in 1929 that Charles

Henry's friend, J. D. Beresford, introduced him to Esme Wynne-Tyson who created Rosamund in that 1911 first run of the play.

It is to *Ash*, which seems to be Vivian's attempt at coming to terms with his unhappy childhood, that we can turn for some idea of the conditions suffered by the children of James Henry Cannell. While *Ash* does, in the main, actually fit many known events and follows a provable time-scale of those events, one has to be careful of taking it absolutely literally. However, the attitudes and emotions of Charles Henry and his siblings are clearly demonstrated within its pages.

Of his father, Charles Henry was scathing:

'As a father, he was an utter failure. He made no attempt to govern nor even to influence his children, and all that they gained from him was just that which the audience gains from the awful example whom the temperance lecturer exhibits. Their mother taught them, guided them, prayed with them and for them, and to her alone they owned that which they had and were. She was a gentle little woman who had been very pretty; among the poor people of the village she was held in far greater respect than mere station could have brought her, and even the clergy, whom her husband attacked with such bitterness, honoured her for the grave fight she made against long odds and without the help that should have been hers by right.'[18]

The reference to the attack on Anglican clergy was a reference to ideas that emanated from James Henry's strict Methodism. He blamed the tithe system, whereby the Anglican clergy had by right a percentage of a farm's revenue, for his own failure as a tenant farmer. In fact, he had 'a bee in his bonnet' about tithes. Many farmers, and not just Nonconformist farmers, disliked the tithe system and throughout the nineteenth century there was a campaign to abolish the system.

Charles Henry goes on to compare his mother's character favourably with his father:

'Against Alston's inconsistency, there was his wife's strength; against his intermittent violence, her gentleness; against his folly, her wisdom. The contrasts might be multiplied indefinitely, and to these contrasts Elizabeth came [back], in her eleventh year...'[19]

He does make an attempt to understand his father's motivations:

'The trouble with John Alston was a lack of cause and effect; he could never realise that man lives by continuous effort, not that he who tilts at windmills should confine such a recreation to spare time, and not make a business of it. His windmill was the iniquity of compelling a Nonconformist farmer to pay tithes, and his lance was a pen. He wrote to papers, and when they refused to publish his bitter and libellous communications he published pamphlets at his own expense; there was, in that time of agricultural depression, a very general feeling that the church bled the land unduly—in some agricultural districts that feeling was very strong indeed—and if Alston had had the business instinct he might have won such notoriety as attends on a Socialist leader of our own time. But he was headstrong, intolerant of compromise, strictly honest, and capricious even in the attacks on his windmill—he had neither the steadiness of purpose nor the tact for a leader, even in a small way.

'When he married, his father had promised him certain financial assistance, and in failing to keep the promise had saddled him with debts that a good businessman might have overcome, even in those bad years of farming. But Alston devised schemes as impracticable as brilliant, in the intervals of attacking the tithe-receiving clergy; and the debts grew heavier instead of lighter, until the tenancy of the farm in which he had begun his married life was exchanged for that of half the size . . .'[20]

That James Henry and his family remained at Forster's Farm until 1888 is certain from *Kelly's Directories*. After that he and his family vanish abruptly from the village. Oral folklore among some of the Cannells has been that James Henry, having made an utter disaster of his tenant farming, then quarrelled with his father, John Cannell (who died in 1894), over what he saw as being denied his rightful inheritance, and had departed from Bedingham never to contact his relatives again. However, James Henry's younger brother John George, who died on December 26 1920, having been a successful farmer at Lane Farm, in Ilketshall St Margaret, Suffolk, not far from Bedingham, seemed to have kept an eye on his brother's fortunes.

John George appears to have been close to his elder 'ne'er-do-well' brother and when he married his wife Maria they had named one of their sons James Henry after him. It was this second James Henry who compiled a family tree and knew that *Ash* was a biographical novel. And it was from this James Henry that his son Frank G. Cannell picked up much of the family oral tradition. Frank comments: 'While my father was alive I can remember him talking about a cousin who had taken the name of Charles Vivian as a writer. Nobody seemed to know much about his life as he had never kept in contact with our family.'[21]

There is no trace of James Henry in the period immediately after he left Bedingham which was sometime after the year 1888. It is not until four years later that he and his family appear in Great Horkesley, in Essex, on a small holding which would agree entirely with Vivian's fictional account in *Ash*. The family were not in Great Horkesley at the time of the 1891 census but seemed to have arrived either late in 1891 or in 1892. According to *Ash*, confirming the family tradition of Elizabeth Rosamund being sent away to be looked after by her maternal grandparents in Mattishall, at the time of the birth of 'Iris' (Olive Louise) 'Mrs Alston' was unwell and not able to cope, needing an operation. The eldest child 'Beth' (Elizabeth Rosamond Eliza) was sent to Grandma and Grandpa Street (Tooley) in Mattishall, to stay until the family could manage once again.

Great Horkesley was a village whose population in 1891 numbered 783. It was separated from Suffolk by the river Stour and was just four miles from Colchester. The local squire was Captain Edward Barrington Purvis Kelso RN, DL, JP, whose residence was Horkesley Park. Apart from Kelso, most of the farms and lands were owned by the Earl Cowper, Lord Ashburton, Messrs J. Pertwee and William Page and a Miss Lawson. Frank Cannell recalled his father telling him that James Henry had arrived at Great Horkesley with still enough funds to sub-rent a three acre small-holding from Herbert Page of Ridgnalls Farm. Page was a local cattle dealer as well as a farmer whose relatives also ran the local post office and owned the nearby Lodge Farm.

Once James Henry and his family had settled on the small holding in Great Horkesley, Elizabeth Rosamond was sent for and returned to live with the rest of the family. In *Ash* 'Beth' returns when she was eleven years old. Elizabeth Rosamond was eleven years old in 1892. Another fact, confirming that we may place some trust in *Ash* as biography, is that Beth mentions Grandpa Street's death occurring just before she rejoins her family. Grandpa Tooley did, in fact, die in 1892, aged 79, in the Forehoe District of Norfolk. Grandma Tooley was to die in 1903, aged 80 years, at Henstead, Norfolk.

Beth returned home from Grandmother Street. At the time of her return, there was a reasonable prospect of affairs righting themselves, in spite of rather than because of any effort on Alston's part. Mrs Alston ever planning and self-sacrificing to the one end of 'getting straight' had fully recovered from her operation, and as far as a woman may she made up for her husband's lack of elementary common sense.[22]

'Beth', had been sent away when 'Clifford' was about five years of age and so he had only vague memories of her while 'Iris' did not know her at all. 'Beth' was encouraged to take up piano and singing and was eventually sent to study in Norwich under a man named Grant. She took her Licentiate of the Royal Academy of Music and begins teaching in schools. Frank Cannell recalls that Elizabeth Rosamond became 'a singer of some repute'.[23] There is a Cannell family tradition of Elizabeth Rosamond having to walk several miles to attend her music lessons. Vivian's daughter recalled: 'I do, but only vaguely, remember learning about a Roselin / Rosalynd who used to walk a great distance for music lessons. What became of her I do not know.'[24]

Frank Cannell recalls that, according to the Cannell family tradition, all three Cannell children were sent to the local National School in Great Horkesley, built in 1873, where 113 local children received their basic education. The mistress at the school was a Miss Page, who was related to James Henry's landlord.

James Henry was not long at Great Horkesley before he had moved again. Once more his indolence and 'chip on the shoulder', whereby he felt the world owed him a living, had caused the small holding to fail as a means of income and support for his family. He now took his family to Blackheath, today a suburb of Colchester. Blackheath was then one of a group of tiny hamlets a few miles to south-east of Colchester. From 1890 it had been regarded as part of the parish of Fringinhoe, four miles from Colchester. Blackheath actually lay two miles to the north of Fringinhoe. Confusingly, Blackheath was regarded for civil administration in the parish of East Donyland while all letters had to be addressed to Colchester.

Again, in *Ash*, this move is faithfully recorded by Vivian when he says that their new home 'meant the vicinity of a big garrison town not fifty miles from London'.[25] This is, of course, an accurate description of Colchester. It is clear that James Henry, according to Cannell family tradition, had long since given up any idea of farming for himself. James Henry Cannell, had now run out of the money provided by Louisa. He went back to being a farm labourer, working on the farm of a George Page, who appears to have been related to Herbert Page of Great Horkesley. It may well have been that the job was the reason for the move to the area and that Herbert Page, James Henry's landlord at Great Horkesley, had taken pity on the Cannell family and recommended James Henry as a labourer on his relative's farm at Fingrinhoe.

It was at Blackheath that the Cannell children finished their unsettled schooling at the mixed National School where George With was head master. There was an average attendance of 79 pupils here. If we continue to accept *Ash* as an accurate record, Elizabeth Rosamond went on to finish her music studies elsewhere. 'Beth', according to the book, finishes her studies in Norwich to which she had to walk, an impossibility from Blackheath. But Norwich might have been used as a cipher for the nearer town of Colchester which would be a walk of three miles or so; far enough but more acceptable than the distance from Blackheath to Norfolk! In *Ash*, 'Beth' certainly begins her career teaching music in Colchester, to the children of army officers and their wives, presumably from the local garrison.

Charles Henry, now having left school, also went to work. All we know of this period is that when he joined the Army he informed the recruiting officer that he had been working as a clerk somewhere in Colchester. That he did not have an adequate education we learn from his Army Record, and the fact that he made some attempts to get some School Certificates while serving in Calcutta. Under the 1870 state system, young Charles Henry would probably have left school when he was fourteen years old. How he occupied his time between the ages of fourteen and eighteen is unclear.

That life at the Cannell home was still not pleasant for the children is expressed in *Ash,* where Charles Henry has 'Beth' as hating 'every circumstance that stood between her and her music and because of that went isolated from her home life'. As for Charles Henry himself, 'Clifford wanted a life other than that which he lived'.[26] James Henry, with his strict Methodism, would doubtless have insisted his children attending the one Wesleyan Chapel in the area in the adjacent village of Rowhedge. The picture that comes over is that of a miserable household with an indolent, impecunious, dogmatic and sometimes violent father, bitter at his lot in life; with a brave struggling mother who had seen the disappearance of her tidy fortune wasted by her husband's profligate attitudes, and who could not protect herself nor her children from her husband's excesses. From 1901, the Census indicates that Louise Anne Cannell had finally separated from her husband and was living elsewhere. The evidence from 1909 shows that she was living with her youngest daughter, Olive, who had then become a schoolteacher in the Gravesend area of Kent, leaving James Henry in Essex.

Coming from what seemed an unhappy background, Charles Henry decided, one November day in 1900, to make that change in his life that he so desperately wanted and he did so with a grand, dramatic gesture.

Vivian's daughter recalled: 'After a family disagreement (nature and date unknown) he changed this (his name) to Evelyn Charles Vivian... He ran away aged about sixteen to join the Army, and fought in the cavalry in the Boer War.'[27]

On Friday, November 15 1900, a young man giving his name as

'Evelyn Henry Vivian', presented himself to the recruiting staff sergeant at Colchester, seeking to enlist in the Corps of Dragoons. He gave his age as twenty years and two months, his trade or calling as a clerk, and his birthplace as Bedingham. The doctor, Dr Taylor, noted that he was 5ft. 9 7/8ths ins. tall, weighed 140 lbs, had a 36 ins. waist and was of fresh complexion, with blue eyes and dark brown hair. He had no distinctive marks. Poignantly enough, no religious denomination was entered for the record. Charles Henry might have already rejected the religious dogma of his father and wanted no part of religion. He was passed as fit for service in the Corps of Dragoons and attested on Sunday, November 17. The signature of 'Evelyn Henry Vivian' on the form is rather nervously written, the letters tight and not evenly formed, as if it was being written for the first time.[28] Indeed, it was.

In *The Woman Tempted Me* (1909) Vivian, as we must now call him, describes how a character, Roy Winton, escapes from his family and joins a cavalry regiment by giving a false name. It is undoubtedly of himself that he is writing:

'The recruiting sergeant was old and short and fat and very ugly. The possible recruit was young, tall and thin, and wore a dirty cycling suit in which he had slept part of the preceding night, under a haystack, and this happened in November. That was why the suit was dirty.

'Your name?' the recruiting sergeant asked.

'Roy Henry Vane.'

The sergeant looked up from the attestation papers a little stunned by the clear, unaccented English.'[29]

The greatest mystery is that when Vivian was asked to give the name and address of his next of kin he gave the name of Daisy West of 68 Station Road, Colchester. A West family did occupy that address in Station Road during the period 1892-1902. Indeed, there were only three other Wests in Colchester and none of them ever lived in Station Road which was variously called Station Road and North Station Road. Therefore we may be sure which West family young Charles Cannell was referring to when he wrote the name,

John Enoch West and his family lived at No. 5, then 68 and then at 72. John Enoch West was a carpenter-journeyman from Stepney, London. He had married Helen Cook of Bures, Essex. They had three daughters; Helen West, born in 1885; Gertie born in 1886 and Daisy born on May 1, 1890. So this Daisy West of 68 Station Road, claimed as Vivian's next of kin, was, in fact, only ten years and six months old at this time.

There are numerous questions that flood the mind but, alas, in spite of a diligent search for any descendants of Daisy West or her sisters, nothing has come to light which might resolve the mystery as to why the eighteen year old youth, on joining the army, gave the name of an unrelated ten year old girl as his next-of-kin. Throughout his fiction the name 'West' crops up several times for various characters. What becomes very clear, reading Vivian's works, is his constant use of names that obviously have meaning for him. Even his publishers and close friends were not immune from having their names used for various fictional characters.

Unsolved, therefore, is the mystery of the triggering mechanism which prompted young Charles Henry Cannell to run away from home and join the cavalry at that particular moment in time. That his home life was an unhappy one, there can be no doubt. But Charles Henry was not a schoolboy but eighteen years old when he left home. It could be that it was simply one row too many between father and son.

According to Vivian's daughter, her father always insisted the reason for his departure was a 'terrible row' with his father.[30] The general idea of a row with his father as a point for leaving home occurs frequently in Vivian's fiction. The closest example occurs in *The Woman Tempted Me*. The son of a character named Hartway returns home from school one day and tells his father that he wishes to make the Army his profession.

'Hartway senior spoke in unmeasured terms of beggarly lieutenants and the expense they involved on their families.'[31] The father wishes the boy to enter the family business and finally commands the boy to 'shut up' concerning his own wishes. 'But the boy, equally self-willed with his father, enlisted as a private in a cavalry regiment, refused to be bought out, and announced his intention of gaining a commission from the ranks. When he found out his mistake he was too proud to acknowledge it.' Needless to say, Charles Henry's own father had no business. Nor would he, as a farm labourer, have had any money to buy a commission for his son had he wanted to. And nor, according to Army records, did young Charles Henry have sufficient education at that time to qualify to receive a commission. This, then, was not the cause of the row young Charles Henry had with his father.

In the novel *Ash* Charles Henry's *alter ego* 'Clifford' goes through an unhappy love affair with a character called 'Eva Fulton', a friend of his sister 'Beth', which ends in early November. Had Daisy West have been six or seven years older than she was, one might have made a piece of logical speculation. 'Clifford's' abrupt departure into the army without informing anyone follows logically on from the unhappy affair with 'Eva Fulton'. The unhappy love affair deflects readers into thinking this was the sole reason for 'Clifford's' departure into the Army. Does it also apply to Charles Henry?

Perhaps a more important point is that, Charles Henry's mother had separated at this time from his father and this event could well have brought matters to a head. Yet nowhere has Vivian brought himself to write about the parental separation and we only have a glimpse of his mother as an extremely sympathetic character in *Ash*. When Louise Anne Cannell died in 1929, she was still living separately from her husband in Kent, while James Henry Cannell, who died in 1931, was living in Essex.

We can only speculate, infuriating as mere speculation is, on that triggering mechanism. The fact is recounted in *Ash* in this manner:

'In mid-November Clifford vanished for a week or more, and then Beth learned that he had joined the Army and was going out to South Africa. This upset her badly, for in growing up to womanhood she had grown human, too, and she had a very real love for Clifford. She grieved over his going just as his mother grieved, and had no other companionship outside the school to lighten her sense of loss.'[32]

The next mystery we must deal with is the choice of Charles Henry Cannell's new names—Evelyn Henry Vivian. Obviously the middle name Henry was in order to keep something of himself although his first name Charles eventually had to reassert itself later. Vivian's daughter believed 'Vivian was the name of a Cornish branch of his family' but the Cannells had no such connection.[33] However, the name Vivian is, perhaps, easy to decipher. Major-General Sir Richard Hussey Vivian (1776-1842), created Baron Vivian in 1841, was one of the ablest cavalry tacticians of his day. He had been handsome, flamboyant and a hero at Waterloo. Every Victorian schoolboy knew about him as they did Wellington or Gordon of Khartoum. He had written a famous book on cavalry tactics. This Vivian was, indeed, a member of the famous Cornish Vivian family. The name is often given as Vyvyan. The legend being that the name derives from the word *chuyvyan*, i.e. 'to escape', for the first Vyvyan was said to have escaped on horse when Lyonesse was submerged. General Vivian later represented his native Truro in the House of Commons. What better name to give when joining the cavalry than that of the most famous cavalry tactician?

Perhaps the most telling point is that as a Privy Councillor, Vivian took a lead in the debate on tithes and wrote a book *Opinions on Tithes* on whether the Anglican Church should continue to be entitled to tithes from farmers, especially farmers who were not Anglicans but Nonconformists. Cornwall itself was strongly Nonconformist and, indeed, Methodist.[34] This volume would surely have had a place on the bookshelves of James Henry, especially with his interest and own complaints on the subject. Young Charles Henry may well have read both Vivian's books.

The coincidence is enough to reasonably argue that it was General Vivian's name which Charles Henry borrowed.

But why Evelyn? In *Ash* 'Clifford' has an unhappy love affair with an 'Eva Fulton' before he joins the army. The names Evelyn, Eve and Eva crop up rather too frequently for random choice in Vivian's novels, and are names usually reserved for characters engaged in unhappy romances. For example, take the heroine Eve in *City of*

Wonder (1923) or Eve in *Arrested* (1949). Is it possible that Charles Henry had such an unhappy affair with a girl called Eve or Eva? Was Evelyn, which can be used by either male or female, and, furthermore, which is a diminutive of the name Eva, adopted for symbolic effect by an intensely romantic, unhappy young man?

Charles Henry Cannell had now taken a most important step in changing his life, the first step on the road to his new identity as Evelyn Charles Vivian.

Notes

1. *A Farmer's Year.* H. Rider Haggard, Longmans, Green & Co, 1899. pp. 4–7. See also index for Moat Farm.
2. *Ibid.*
3. *The Personal Names of the Isle of Man*, J. J. Kneen, Oxford University Press, 1937.
4. Letter to author from Frank E. Cannell, November 26, 1991. One of the most enthusiastic sources who put me in touch with many Cannell family members was Dr Ruth Hadman of the Old Vicarage, Bedingham who is the local historian. She was able to supply me with details of Census returns in the village and sort out the large number of Cannells. I am also grateful to information supplied by D. Cannell of Beccles, Suffolk, Miss A.M. Walton MBE, the daughter of Agnes Mabel Cannell of Aldeburgh and Joyce Bond of Lowestoft, also a Cannell descendant. The collective folk memories have helped to put some speculative flesh on an area which would have otherwise remained blank. Basic facts of the whereabouts of James Cannell and his family, and his occupation, were confirmed by Census returns and *Kelly's Directory's*. And I should further acknowledge a debt of help from H. Rider Haggard's grandson, Commander Mark Cheyne RN (Ret'd) of Ditchingham. Also of help was a letter from Ben Burgess MBE, Dip.Ag.(Cantab.), FRAS, FIAgrE, of Ben Burgess & Co, Norwich, whose grandfather and father used to farm in Bedingham in the late 19th Century—letter to author May 22, 1994.
5. Frank Cannell to author, November 26, 1991.

6. 'John Wesley and Mann,' Jessie Kerruish, Mannin, No 9, p. 516.
7. Letter to author October 24, 1991.
8. *The Illustrated London News: Social History of Victorian England*, Christopher Hibbert, Angus and Robertson, London, 1975 – p. 60.
9. Information gathered from Census Rolls and Certificates of Births, Deaths and Marriages, St Catherine's House, London.
10. Marriage, Death Certificates and Will.
11. Census Rolls.
12. *Ash*, Charles Cannell, Hutchinson, 1925.
13. *A Farmer's Year* (see above) p. 7/8.
14. Ben Burgess, letter to author, May 22, 1994.
15. *The Illustrated London News*: (above) p. 67.
16. Ben Burgess (above).
17. Frank E. Cannell to author, November 26, 1991.
18. *Ash* (above) pp. 61/63.
19. *Ibid.*
20. *Ibid.*
21. Frank Cannell to author, November 26, 1991.
22. *Ash* (above) pp. 61/63.
23. Frank Cannell to author, November 26, 1991.
24. Mrs Katharine Ashton to author, January 13, 1992.
25. *Ash*, see above, p. 139.
26. *Ash*, see above, p. 134.
27. Mrs Katharine Ashton to author, April 24, 1990.
28. Public Record Office, WO 97/6137 XC 197528, Army record of Evelyn Henry Vivian.
29. *The Woman Tempted Me*, E. Charles Vivian, Andrew Melrose, London, 1909. p. 14.
30. Mrs Katharine Ashton to author, April 23, 1990.
31. *The Woman Tempted Me.* as above, p. 4/5.
32. *Ash*, as above, p. 129.
33. Mrs Katharine Ashton to author, September 24, 1991.
34. *Opinions on Tithes*, Sir Richard Hussey Vivian, J. Ridgeway, London, 1833.

CHAPTER TWO

THE ARMY YEARS

Two days after his recruitment in Colchester, Private 5435 'Evelyn Henry Vivian' reported to the depot of the Corps of Dragoons at Shorncliffe in Kent. In his novel *The Woman Tempted Me* (1909), it is clear that Vivian is talking of his own feelings when he records those of 'Roy Henry Vane' who has just joined the army in similar circumstances.

'He knew it was a second birth, practically, for all the old things of life had ceased to be, as far as he was concerned. Today he commenced another life, different from any he had known, with everything to learn, everything new; and he was glad of that for he wanted nothing left to influence him. Perhaps with this beginning he could live true, keep white, he told himself. He did not dream of glory or promotion, or Victoria Crosses, for he did not want this. Only to start again with no habit or association kept from the preceding days, and to live this life out to its end, alone. Most of all he wanted to be alone.'[1]

It is to the vivid passages in his 1914 account *The British Army from Within* that we may turn to get some glimpses of Vivian's career. One passage is remarkably close to one in *The Woman Tempted Me* and this describes the arrival at the Shorncliffe cavalry depot. It is clearly a piece of autobiographical writing.

'He went up a hill, and along a muddy lane, and, arriving at the barracks, inquired, as he had been told to, for the quarter-master sergeant of C Squadron. He was directed to the quarter-master sergeant's office, and, in arrival there, was asked his name and the nature of his business by a young corporal who took life as a joke and regarded recruits as a special form of food for his amusement. Having ascertained the name of the recruit, the corporal, who was a kindly fellow at heart, took him down to the regimental coffee bar and provided him with a meal of cold meat, bread and coffee—at the squadron's expense, of course, for the provision of the meal was a matter of duty. The corporal then indicated the room in which the recruit was to sleep, and left him.

'The recruit opened the door of the room, and looked in. It was a long room, with a row of narrow beds down each side, and in the middle of it two tables on iron trestles, whereupon were several basins. On almost every bed sat a man, busily engaged in cleaning some article of clothing or equipment; some were cleaning buttons, some were pipe-claying belts, some were engaged with sword hilts and brick dust, some were cleaning boots—all were cleaning up as if their lives depended on it, for 'lights out' would be sounded at a quarter past ten, and it was already past nine o'clock. When they saw the recruit, they gave him greeting. "Here's another one!" they cried. "Here's another victim!" and other phrases which led the particular recruit to think, quite erroneously, that he had come to something very bad indeed. Two or three were singing, with more noise than melody, a song which was very old when Queen Anne died—it was one of the ditties of the regiment—sung by its men on all possible and most impossible occasions. One man shouted to the recruit that he had "better flap before he drew issue"; and that he could not understand at all. Translated into civilian language, it meant that he had better desert before he exchanged his civilian clothing for regimental attire, but this he learned later. They seemed a jolly crowd, very fond of flavouring their language with words which, in civilian estimation, were terms of abuse, but passed as common currency here.

'The recruit stood wondering—out of all these beds, there seemed to be no bed for him. After a minute or two, however, the corporal in charge of the room came up to him, and pointed him to a bed in one corner of the room; its usual occupant was on guard for twenty-four hours, and the recruit was informed that he could occupy the bed for the night. In the morning he could go to the quartermaster sergeant's stores and draw blankets, sheets, a pillow and 'biscuits' for his own use. After that, he would be allotted a bed-cot to himself. Biscuits, it must be explained, are square mattresses of coir,' (the prepared fibre of the husk of the coco-nut often used for making ropes and matting) 'of which three placed end to end form a full-sized mattress for a military cot.

'Sitting on the borrowed bed cot, the recruit was able to take a good look round. The wags of these men, the quickness in cleaning and polishing articles of equipment, were worth watching, he decided. They joked and chaffed each other, they sung scraps of songs, allegedly pathetic and allegedly humorous; they shouted from one end of the room in order to carry on conversations; they called the Army names, they called each other names, none of them complimentary, they made a lot of noise, and in that noise one of them, having finished his cleaning, slept; when he snored, one of his comrades threw a boot at him and, since the boot hit him, he woke up and looked around, but in vain. Therefore he calmly went to sleep again, but this time he did not snore- The recruit, who had come out of an ordinary civilian home, and hitherto had had only the vaguest notions as to what the Army was really like, wondered if he were dreaming, and then realised that he himself was one of these men, since he had voluntarily given up certain years of his life to this business. With that reflection he undressed and got into bed. After "lights out" had sounded and been promptly obeyed, he went to sleep . . .'[2]

In *The Woman Tempted Me*, 'Roy Henry Vane', having arrived at the depot in precisely this way, meets an old soldier within a day of two of his arrival who offers to sell him some kit. 'Roy Henry Vane' does not realise that this is against regulations and the old hand merely wants the money for alcohol. When the sergeant-major demands to know where the kit is, the old soak says it has been stolen. 'Roy Henry Vane' is accused of the theft and brought before the colonel and given 168 hours imprisonment with hard labour. Had this happened to Vivian at this time it would have been placed on his record. The evidence is that Vivian was a model soldier and showed early promise being appointed a lance-corporal after just six months on July 5 1901.[3]

Life was not arduous at the Shorncliffe depot with the '3rd Provisional Regiment of Dragoons', under the command of Major H.W. Munro. This 'home posting' lasted a total of one year and eight days. Again from *The British Army from Within* we glimpse a little of what life was like for young Vivian at the depot.

'Grooming in a cavalry regiment is a meticulous business, the writer has personal knowledge of and acquaintance with a troop office who used to make his morning inspection of the troop horses with white kid gloves on, and the horses were supposed to be groomed to such a state of cleanliness that when the officer rubbed the skin the wrong way his gloves remained unsoiled. Such a state of perfection as this, of course, is possible in barracks, and it is hardly necessary to say that the officer in question was not exactly idolised by his men. Like most youth fresh from Sandhurst, he was incapable of making allowances.'[4]

One other matter concerning his army service on which Vivian seems to dwell on is that of 'gentlemen rankers'. In those days, in England's structured class system, one could find the unusual spectacle of members of the upper and middle classes enlisting in the ranks. One could be a 'gentleman' without being an 'officer'. One wonders if Vivian now considered himself a 'gentleman ranker'? Was he already disguising his unhappy childhood? We know he later claimed that his father was a 'gentleman farmer' rather than an agricultural labourer. It is hard to know what fantasy world he entered when he adopted the name of General Lord Vivian's family. From his daughter's recollection, Vivian still claimed relation to this Cornish military family many years later. Was he trying to pretend to his fellow soldiers that he was a 'gentleman ranker'? It is possible. Though one would think that his educational background and lack of private income would have rendered this a difficult fantasy.

'There is in the cavalry a greater percentage of gentleman rankers than in any other branch of the service, and there are more queer histories attaching to men in cavalry regiments than in any of the other arms. The gentleman ranker usually shakes down to a level with the rest of the regiment. It has never yet come within the writer's knowledge that any officer accorded to a gentleman ranker received different treatment from that enjoyed by the majority of the men, in spite of the assertions of melodrama writing on the subject. Favouritism in the cavalry, as in any branch of the service, is fatal to discipline, and is not indulged in to any great extent, certainly not to the benefit of gentleman rankers as a whole. Work and officers stand first; social niceties in civilian life count for nothing, and the gentleman ranker who joins the services with a view to a commission must prove himself fitted to hold it from a military point of view.

'The gentleman ranker is frequently a remittance man, and in that case he is certain of many friends, for the frequenters of the canteen are usually short of money a day or two before pay-day comes, and thus the man with a well-lined pocket is of material use to them. Disinterested friendships, however, are too common in the Army to call for comment and many and many a case occurs of one cavalryman, quick at his work, helping another at cleaning saddlery or equipment after he has finished his own, without hope of reward.'[5]

In South Africa, Britain's war against the Boer republics was still in progress. The war had been provoked by Britain after the discovery of gold in Transvaal's Witwatersrand. The war had started on October 11, 1899, and after some initial Boer successes, by July 4, 1900, British forces had defeated the Boer conventional forces and occupied all the major Boer cities and townships, but the Boers then turned to guerrilla warfare. The new commander-in-chief of the Army in South Africa, Lord Horatio Kitchener, had started a new, ruthless policy of not only attempting to capture Boer combatants but rounding up women and children and placing them in concentration camps, the first use of the concept made notorious by Nazi Germany. Some 130,000 women and children were kept in these special camps in which, in the space of a year, 26,000 were to die of privations suffered. Still the Boers fought on with a desperation and Kitchener eventually sought reinforcements to bring British forces in South Africa to a total of 300,000.[6]

At the end of a year in Shorncliffe, without ever hearing a shot fired in anger, young Vivian was told to embark with reinforcements for South Africa to join the 7th Dragoon Guards known as 'The Black Horse', which have achieved the epithet in South Africa as 'The Lucky 7th' because it had managed to come moderately unscathed through several fierce engagements.[7]

The 7th had their home quarters at Norwich which may or may not have been a reason for the dispatch of the young Norfolk lad to join it. The 7th were part of the 4th Cavalry Brigade and, commanded by Lieutenant Colonel W.H.M. Lowe they had sailed for the South African war in February, 1900, with a strength of 24 officers and 565 NCOs and men and 506 horses. They were immediately thrown into the main theatre of war as part of Kitchener's force advancing on the Boer stronghold of Prieska. They had seen major actions at Roodikop, Zand River, Klip River, Diamond Hill and Onderste Port.

Young Vivian joined his regiment on November 23, 1901. It was then in the vicinity of the border between the Cape Colony and the Orange Free State, its movements extremely fluid. It was engaged in wearisome sweeps, seeking out Boer guerrilla commandos, and making cordons to keep the local population suitably cowed. In that month of November the 14,000 British troops in the Orange Free State had only been able to capture 30 Boers suspected of being guerrillas. December saw the 7th in a brigade with the 3rd Dragoon Guards, the King's Dragoon Guards and the 6th Mounted Infantry, commanded by Colonel de Lisle, patrolling the blockhouse line between Kroonstadt and Harrismith. The efforts of tracking down and attempting to capture Boer leaders, such as Christiaan de Wet, was a hard task. On one day the regiment had to ride 58 miles in a fruitless search and on another a further 47 miles. It was exhausting to men and horses.[8]

But it was not just police work. On December 8, 1901, Captain Gage, commanding the 7th advance guard, came under heavy fire from a flanking kopje or hill. Because the cavalrymen's swords had been withdrawn, due to the nature of their work, Gage ordered his men to fix bayonets and use them as lances to disperse the Boers from their position. Again, on December 28, Major Charles William Thompson, the second-in-command of the regiment, commanding a combined patrol of 600 men, came under heavy shell and pom-pom fire and a cavalry charge was ordered against the Boer positions with fixed bayonets. Thompson was subsequently awarded the Distinguished Service Order, the highest decoration won by a member of the regiment during the war.[9]

The regiment, in its sweeps, moved north from the Cape Colony and Orange Free State border on to the Modder River, during this period. In *The British Army from Within*, Vivian recounts an interesting story of this time which clearly shows his early eye for the weird.

'While on the subject of camping, there is one more yarn of South Africa and the war which merits telling, although it only concerns a bad case of "nerves". It happened during the last year of the war that a column crossed the Modder River from south to north, going in the direction of Brandfort and the camp was pitched to the right just to the north of the Glen Drift. At this point in its intercourse, the Modder River runs between steep, cliff-like banks, from which a belt of mimosa scrub stretches out for nearly a quarter of a mile on each side of the river. After camp had been pitched for the night, the sentries round about the camp were finally posted with a special view to guarding the drift, and northward front of the column, and its flanks. Only two of these sentries, however, were considered necessary to protect the rear, which rested on the impenetrable belt of mimosa scrub along the bank.

'One of these sentries along the scrub came on duty at midnight, just after the moon had gone down. He took over; from the sentry who preceded him on the post, and started to keep watch according to orders, though in his particular position there was little enough to watch. Quite suddenly he grew terrible afraid, not with a natural kind of fear, but with the nightmarish kind of terror that children are known to experience in the dark. His reason told him that in the position that he occupied there was nothing which could possibly harm him, for behind him was the bush, through which a man could not even crawl, while before him and to either side was the chain of sentries, of which he formed a part, surrounding his sleeping comrades. His imagination, however, or possibly his instinct, insisted that something uncanny and evil was watching him from the darkness of the tangled mimosa bus, and was waiting a chance to strike at him in some horrible fashion. He tried to shake off the childish fear, to assure himself that it could not possible be other than a trick of "nerves" brought on by darkness and the need for keeping watching, when—crash!—something struck him with tremendous force in the back and sent him forward on his face.

'Half-stunned, he picked himself up from the ground, and the pain in his back was sufficient to assure him that he had not merely fallen asleep and imagined the whole business. With his loaded rifle at the ready he searched the edge of the mimosa bush as closely as he was able, but could discover nothing; he had an idea of communicating with the sentry next in line to himself, but since there was no further disturbance, and he decided to say nothing, but simply to stick to his post until the next relief came round.

'Suddenly the uncanny sense of terror returned to him, intensified. He felt this time that the evil thing which had struck him before would strike again, and he felt certain that he was being watched by unseen eyes. He was new to the country, as an irregular he was new to military ways, and he promised himself that if ever he got safely home he would not volunteer for active service again. The sense of something unseen and watching him grew, and with it grew also the nightmarish terror, until he was actually afraid to move, then, by means of the same mysterious agency, he was struck again to the ground, and this time he lay only partially conscious and quite helpless until the reliefs came round. The sergeant in charge of the reliefs had an idea at first of making the man a close prisoner for lying down and sleeping at his post, but after a little investigation he changed his mind and sent one of his men for the doctor instead.

'The doctor announced, after examination, that if the blow which felled the man had struck him a few inches higher up on the back, he would not have been alive to remember it, and the man himself was taken into hospital for a few days to recover from the injuries so mysteriously inflicted. In the morning the column moved off on its way, and no satisfactory reason could be adduced for the midnight occurrence.

'But residents in that district will tell you, unto this day, that one who has the patience to keep it and watch in the moonlight, can see big baboons come up from the mimosa scrub and amuse themselves by throwing clods of earth and rock at each other.'[10]

The New Year of 1902 simply continued the interminable drives to find and capture the Boer guerrilla commandos and leaders. 'No form of warfare is so trying to the nerves and temper as that in which an enemy has no definite plan, but continually manoeuvres so as to avoid action, one day in front of one, the next day behind', wrote Captain J. E. D. Holland of the 7th. The fact was that the British army, and the cavalry in particular, were still amateurs at encountering the guerrilla tactics of the Boers and were still trying to engage and fight with set-piece battles.[11]

On February 16, the Boer General Christiaan de Wet was reported with a large commando at Elandskop. The 7th, King's Dragoon Guards, and 6th Mounted Infantry forced march through the night to engage him. After covering the 42 miles in less than six hours they arrived to find de Wet and his commando had vanished.

In March, 1902, however, rumours began of peace talks. In fact the Boer leaders had resigned themselves to capitulation to the superior British forces. They were now trying to negotiate the best terms for their people.

On April 25, Vivian's Regiment, in camp at Willowglen, near Bethlehem, beheld the sight of Christiaan de Wet and his staff ride into their camp under a white flag. Major Thompson, the acting CO of the regiment, in the absence of Colonel Lowe, invited his erstwhile enemy to lunch in the Mess. Captain N. D. H. Campbell recalled that it was a memorable occasion with champagne to celebrate although de Wet took nothing stronger than lime juice.[12]

The war was not yet over and on May 6, the men of the 7th had to fight off a Boer commando of 300 mounted men near Groenvlei, escaping the engagement without a single casualty. Lieutenant W. F. Chappell was ordered to take his troop, with fixed bayonets, and chase a group of fugitives. Five Boers were killed and 130 captured in this the last action of the Black Horse in the war.

On June 1, with Vivian's regiment now encamped at Lindley, in the Kroonstadt district, church parade had just ended when Major Thompson received and read a telegram: 'From Chief, Pretoria, to General Elliott, Lindley. Peace was signed last night'. The Boer War was over. It had taken 450,000 British soldiers three years to subdue 87,000 untrained, part-time irregulars at a cost of 20,700 British lives for only 4,000 enemy dead. 350,000 horses had been slain and the total financial cost to Britain was £220 million.[13]

Vivian's Regiment had lost a total of three officers and 61 other ranks killed. Their names appear on a memorial in Norwich Cathedral, unveiled on November 17, 1904.[14]

The next day, June 2, Captain M. F. Gage, one sergeant, two corporals and six privates of the regiment, were detailed to proceed home to represent the Regiment at the Coronation of King Edward VII.

The 7th were now converted into occupation forces and in March the newly promoted Colonel Thomson became the regiment's CO succeeding Colonel Lowe. On July 7, 1904, the regiment finally left South Africa and was stationed in Canterbury in Kent. But, by then, Vivian was no longer serving with the Black Horse.

On October 23, 1902, Evelyn Henry Vivian was given a new posting to the 5th Dragoon Guards (Princess Charlotte's Own). The regiment was called 'The Green Horse' because of its Irish connections. Vivian had been returned to the rank of private and given a new army number as 4885.[15] The 5th had been badly mauled during the war. It was reduced almost to half-strength and badly needed reinforcements. The part it played in the war was recounted by its commanding officer, Lt. Col. St. John Corbet Gore, in *The Green Horse in Ladysmith*, printed by Sampson Low and Marston & Co, in London, in 1901. By the time Vivian was posted to 'The Green Horse', the bulk of the regiment's surviving 17 officers and 313 other ranks, had already embarked from Durban for Bombay, in India, on the *SS Mohawk* on March 19, 1902. A further 163 NCOs and men were left behind and transferred to the 7th Dragoons. It would appear, therefore, that Vivian's transference was part of a general exchange of men.

Vivian followed the regiment from Bombay to the 5th's base at the garrison town of Lucknow, in Uttar Pradesh which Britain had annexed from its native rulers, the Nawabs of Awadh, in 1856. As well as an army headquarters, the town was a commercial centre with cotton and paper mills, sugar refineries and railway workshops. It was also the town where La Martiniere College was situated which Rudyard Kipling used as a model for St Xavier's in *Partibus* where young Kim is sent for a 'sahib's education' Kipling, who had visited Lucknow for the Pioneer, saw it 'as a peculiarly filthy city' and used Lucknow Railway Station as the scene of a bitter parting.[16]

It was in Lucknow that young Vivian, like Kim, returned to the subject of his poor education.

He had been posted to 'C' Company, commanded by Captain William Quintyne Winwood, then aged 27. Winwood was to become the CO of the regiment in 1914. On November 15, Vivian had received a pay rise for 'good conduct', which went with Good Conduct badges, granted at 2, 5 and 12 year service dates if the recipient had, indeed, served well. The badge was chevrons worn upside down on the left arm and at the lower end of the sleeve. It becomes clear from his service record that young Vivian wanted to make something of himself and having no educational qualifications, he sought to obtain them. At Lucknow he was able to take his Lower Standard Certificate of Education (Part I) on January 27, 1903. At this time Winwood was posted and the adjutant of the regiment,

Captain B. G. Clay also became Vivian's company commander. Vivian now took his 2nd Class Certificate of Education, passing it on December 8, 1903. He also attended several classes of instruction, including riding, swimming and marksmanship, taking certificates of competence, and was deemed by his company commander as being qualified for the rank of corporal. Indeed, he had been appointed unpaid lance-corporal again on October 13, 1903, but was not appointed paid lance-corporal until October 1, 1904. At the same time Vivian was designated as achieving a Special Proficiency Class 1 category which was in recognition of obtaining his Educational Certificates, and his marksmanship and horsemanship qualifications.[17]

The period in Lucknow was obviously idyllic for young Vivian. The Inspector General of Cavalry reported most favourable on the condition of the regiment and training of all ranks.

Then, on February 25, 1904, with a new CO, Lt Col William John Cheshyre Butler, the 5th were ordered to Bombay to embark on RIMS *Clive* to proceed back to South Africa. They arrived at Durban on May 14 and left for Bloemfontein where they were to be stationed. Vivian's record shows that he went with the regiment. Indeed, he seemed quite happy with them and on April 1, just a few weeks after arriving back in South Africa, he asked for his service to be extended for eight years, this meant a further four years active service and four more on the Army Reserve.[18]

Importantly, Vivian now requested that the name of Daisy West, of 68 Station Road, Colchester, be removed as his next of kin, and that of his sister 'Miss Olive Cannell, of Blackheath, Colchester', be placed in his records. The amendment was signed by Captain Clay.[19]

Vivian never rose further than the rank of lance-corporal but he seemed happy enough and was a good steady soldier. He had received the Queen's South Africa Medal for active service with clasps for the Cape Colony, the Orange Free State theatres of war and for the years 1901 and 1902. The idyll seemed to continue. While initial conditions at Bloemfontein were not good, even the officers' mess on the sandy veldt was no more than a tin hut, the regiment was put to work building their base so that when they left they had constructed a series of fine barracks, stables and the officers even had two tennis courts and a garden. Apart from the construction work there were few strenuous tasks for the regiment other than to be reviewed on October 8, 1904, by Field Marshal Earl Roberts, and on January 22, 1906, by HRH the Duke of Connaught and General R. S. S. Baden-Powell.[20]

It was during this period that Vivian discovered his writing talent and began to write. It may be, like Edgar Wallace, that he started his career by selling items to the local South African newspapers and journals. *The Cape Times, Cape Mercury, East London Daily Press, South African Review* and *Eastern Press* had published Wallace. Edgar Wallace had gone to South Africa as a medical orderly and become noticed as 'the soldier poet' for writing verse in the Rudyard Kipling style. In many ways, Vivian's career emulated Edgar Wallace's.

Indeed, in his semi-autobiographical novel *Ash*, on page 142, Vivian seems to confirm the idea that he was already writing pieces of journalism at this time for when he talks of his alter ego Clifford, he records: 'He, for his part, stayed on in the Army after the South African War, went to India with his regiment, returned to Africa and took up some journalistic work there...'

Through 1906 Vivian must also have been spending time on writing his first novel for it was published by the London publisher Gay and Bird in April, 1907. It was called *The Shadow of Christine* and was priced six shillings. Gay and Bird specialised in military publications, although they did a fiction list aimed at the popular end of the market. It is likely that the young soldier sent his manuscript to them because he became familiar with their military books.

It has been claimed by bibliographer W. O. G. Lofts that the book heralded the development of Vivian's later supernatural mysteries.[21] This is wrong. It is a 'serious novel' set in Australia, perhaps a curious choice of location when Vivian had never been there. It is a tale of human passions, a theme that was to become Vivian's standard fare in these 'literary' works. The protagonist is an adventurer, James Derek Winton, and it tells of his entanglement with Christine

White, the daughter of a friend, who believes that she must marry a man whom she is not in love with. A doom ridden fate stalks the tale and there is no resolution. Vivian published his book as 'Evelyn C. H. Vivian'. It was to be the first and last time that he chose this form for most reviewers sprang to the conclusion that 'Evelyn' was a woman.

The *Times Literary Supplement* of April 19, 1907, concluded 'that Miss Evelyn C. H. Vivian is not a mature novelist'. The reviewer points to stylistic anachronisms but the overall conclusion was that the writer had promise. 'The mining town and the Australian desert are as vivid as the people of the story. All is strongly felt and strongly told—real people, real places, real passions; and though Miss Vivian will make advances as she goes . . . it is a pleasure to meet with a story in which its own author has clearly believed and been interested from the beginning to the end.'

The book was published in America, by R. F. Fenno & Co. of New York, on April 9, 1910, in a $1.50 edition. *The New York Times* also made the mistake of thinking Vivian was a woman.

'The tale is more uneven in its workmanship than one often sees. In her desire to be strong the author frequently over paints both character and scenes. The book contains some fine passages and it does not often loosen its hold upon the reader. In the character of Christine, the author had scored a success. The girl's childlike nature, from which a latent womanhood rises to meet a supreme trial; her reticent patience, her unselfish courage, stand out clearly, giving dignity as well as a pathos to a creation in which the author has shown a restraint that the rest of the novel had not led us to expect. Her conception and handling of this character leads us to look with interest for her future work.'[22]

They would look in vain for Evelyn C. H. Vivian, for the future works would be published as E. Charles Vivian.

Nevertheless, the mistake of gender aside, *The Shadow of Christine* had been a success for the 24 year old soldier. He now records that he was writing regularly for *The Friend* newspaper in Bloemfontein. The newspaper had been re-launched in 1896 as *The

Friend and in March, 1900, had been seized by Lord Roberts and changed into a pro-British newspaper mainly for the troops. The services of *The Times* war correspondent Perceval Landon, and other well known journalists such as Howell A. Gwynne and F. W. Buxton helped edit it while Rudyard Kipling and Sir Arthur Conan Doyle contributed to it. If Vivian had joined their company he was successful, indeed.

Perhaps that success went to his head, for Vivian's sober career in the cavalry came to a curious end. He was due for demobilisation in November, 1908, having completed his eight years active service before transference to the Army Reserve and the prospect of a good pension. He was due to leave the regiment at precisely the same time that the 5th were scheduled to leave South Africa. On November 23, 1907, his company commander, the popular Major B. G. Clay had already left with other officers for Ballincollig, Ireland, to form a depot for the 5th. The date set for the final withdrawal from Bloemfontein was to be November 30, 1908, when the regiment was to be replaced by the 6th Dragoon Guards.

On September 14, 1908, Lance-Corporal Vivian, whose career had been so stable and sober, with an accumulation of Good Conduct chevrons, was placed under arrest and taken before a district court martial the following day. Alas, it is typical of the mysteries which surround Vivian that the court martial records have disappeared. However, the result was that Vivian was sentenced to 28 days detention for 'neglecting to obey regimental orders' and stripped of his rank and privileges. He was detained in the regiment's detention barracks from September 15 and returned to duty on October 12, 1908.[23]

What the cause of this lapse was we shall never know. Captain C. Boardman (Ret'd), assistant to the Regimental Secretary of The Royal Dragoon Guards, comments: 'Disobeying Regimental Orders would probably be a failing to be at an appointed place of duty, i.e. Guard, Parade or even a move—almost anything! It was probably related to a night out on the tiles! "28 days" was pretty heavy, but was probably associated with active service.'[24]

A month later Vivian left with the rest of 5th Dragoons en route for Ireland. Because his service was now ended, he disembarked in England on December 30, 1908, and reported to the Discharge Depot at Shorncliffe. On December 31, 1908, he was officially discharged from service having completed seven years and 123 days. He was transferred to the Army Reserve on January 1, 1909.

Vivian was now home again so far as England was his home. He was twenty-six years old, a recipient of a small pension, not as big as he might have received had he not spoilt the end of his service by a court martial, but it was a pension nevertheless together with an army gratuity payment of £20. More importantly, he was now a published author and had also claimed to be writing articles for *The Friend*. He seemed to have no doubt what his next step for a future career should be.

Notes

1. *The Woman Tempted Me; the story of a selfish man*, Andrew Melrose, London, September, 1909. p. 16.
2. *The British Army from Within*, Hodder & Stoughton, November, 1914. pp. 26-28.
3. E.H.Vivian, Service Record, Public Record Office, WO 97/6137 XC 197528.
4. *The British Army from Within*, p. 85.
5. *The British Army from Within*, p. 86-87.
6. *The Crisis of Imperialism*, Richard Shannon, Hart-Davis, MacGribbon, London, 1974, pp. 323-337.
7. *The 4th/7th Royal Dragoon Guards 1685-1980*, T.M. Brereton, published by The Regiment, Catterick, 1982. See Chapter XI; 'On trek with the Black Horse' covering the period 1895-1905, pp. 271-294.
8. *Ibid.*
9. *Ibid.*
10. *The British Army from Within*, p. 115.

11. *The 4th/7th Royal Dragoon Guards* (see above).
12. *Ibid.*
13. *The Crisis of Imperialism* (see above).
14. *The Story of a regiment of Horse, being the Regimental History from 1685 to 1922 of the 5th Princess Charlotte of Wales' Dragoon Guards.* Compiled by Major the Hon. Ralph Legge Pomeroy, some time a Member of the Corps, William Blackwood, Edinburgh, 1924. 2 vols. See pp. 261-263.
15. PRO, WO 97/6137 XC 197528 (as above).
16. *The Strange Ride of Rudyard Kipling: His Life and Works*, Angus Wilson, Seeker & Warburg, London, 1977. p. 92.
17. PRO, WO 97/6137 XC 197528.
18. *Ibid.*
19. *Ibid.*
20. *The Story of a Regiment of Horse* (see above).
21. 'On the Trail of the Mysterious 'Jack Mann'' by W.O.G. Lofts, edited by Robert E. Briney, *Armchair Detective*, 1972. p. 19-22. Curiously, Mr Lofts gives the impression of having read *The Shadow of Christine* by stating 'what a splendid book it is, with a genuinely eerie atmosphere!'
22. *The New York Times*, April 23, 1910.
23. PRO, WO 97/6137 XC 197528.
24. Letter to author, February 3, 1994.

CHAPTER THREE

A Career in Journalism

The first thing Vivian did on arriving back in England, so it appears, was make contact with his family, perhaps to see if there had been changes in their circumstance since he had left home. He went to see his sister Olive first. She had become a schoolteacher and was living with their mother in Gravesend, in Kent. Significantly enough, the first address we have for Vivian in 1913, at the time of his marriage, is Gravesend. Vivian's father was still living an isolated life in Essex although he occasionally saw his younger brother William George at his farm at Ilketshall St Margaret. In this way, this branch of the Cannell family came to know that E. Charles Vivian was, in reality their cousin, Charles Henry Cannell, and learnt of Elizabeth Rosamond's success in her singing career.

In fact, Elizabeth Rosamond, Vivian's eldest sister was now married. She had married at Brentford Register Office on October 14, 1905, giving her address as that of her father at Blackheath, Colchester. One would deduce from this that Elizabeth had opted to stay with her father after her mother had left him. Elizabeth Rosamond had elevated her father's profession to 'gentleman' on her marriage certificate rather than admit the reality of his being a 'farm labourer' working on George Page's farm at Fingrinhoe. It was not the only incorrect information that Elizabeth had given. She put her age down as twenty-one years, instead of nearly twenty-five. She had married Ashford Vincent Clark, a twenty-two year old civil engineer living in Ealing, London. Ashford Clarke was the son of a Somerset farmer, William Clarke of Budleigh Trull, and his wife Gilla, formerly Manning. He had been born on July 21, 1883.[1]

If we accept Vivian's autobiographical novel, *Ash*, Elizabeth, or 'Beth' of the story, while married to Ashford, who actually appears in the novel with very little disguise as an architect named 'Arthur Ashford', was pursuing her musical career in London at this time.

In the novel, she left Ashford after only three weeks of marriage, did well on her own and became a concert singer, staying at London's Grosvenor Hotel. She asked Ashford for a divorce but he refused to give her one. Also, according to the novel, 'Beth' had now adopted the stage name 'Pearl' because she hated her own name. Certainly, at this time, Elizabeth insisted on the use of Rosamund (her birth-given names were actually 'Elizabeth Rosamond Eliza' but she used 'Rosamund' on all later documents, including her will). Vivian's daughter says she came to know her as 'Aunt Diana'. Could 'Diana' have been a stage name?

Vivian describes the reuniting of his alter ego 'Clifford' with 'Beth' in this passage:

'Clifford, back from Africa, came up to the Grosvenor to see his sister; she was out when he arrived—she was, in fact, looking for some place in which to live in London—and he waited near on half a day for her. He was tanned deep brown by sun and wind, and rather shabbily dressed, and Pearl, coming back from her search, did not recognise him at first, while he failed utterly to recognise his sister in this brilliant being.

'They jarred horribly. Clifford had arrived with twenty pounds, and had taken over the care of his parents on an inadequate income; from what he saw of Pearl, she belonged to a different world from his, and he resented this appearance of prosperity while he himself had to pinch and plan, economising every penny. He had not gained the breadth of view that came to him from later experiences and was inclined to judge from externals, with the rigid uncompromising judgment of youth. And Iris had told him of Pearl's marriage with Ashford.

"When are you going back to him?" he asked.

Pearl shook her head. "That gateway is closed," she said. "I shall never go back."

"He's a good man," Clifford urged, "and you're his wife."

"I know he's a good man—that's the hurt of it," she said. "But I have set out to make good with my voice, just as you have set out to make good by writing, and I must go my own way."

'To Clifford, that way meant expensive hotels and fine clothes—he could not comprehend how she had slaved and planned to win just thus far, nor on how insecure a point she stood then, with just one concert success behind her. There was bitten into him the knowledge that, in the days lying just behind his return, his parents had known the extreme of poverty—while Pearl went her way unheeding, for all that he knew. He put out of his mind an unjust suspicion that entered it but still he could not forgive.'[2]

While Vivian refers to 'parents' in the plural, he never specifically mentions the father again. There is, however, another incident in *Ash* which is worthy of attention.

'One day—it was after the second concert, which virtually assured her place in the first rank, she went down to the home to which Clifford had moved his parents. Iris was there on a brief holiday, having gone out teaching, and Iris welcomed her and was glad of her success, knowing how she had worked for it in the years Clifford spent away from England. They were all glad, save Clifford, who came home from a hard and disappointing day in London, an hour or more before it was time for her to go back.'[3]

Where *Ash* does depart from the reality is that 'Beth/Pearl' becomes ill with tuberculosis, and has to give up her singing career. She retires to Wood Bay in the Linton/Lynmouth area of Devon where, at the end of the novel, she dies alone, steadfastly refusing to go back to her husband, Ashford.

In reality, Elizabeth did contract tuberculosis and had to give up singing.[4] But she did not die. Instead she went back to Ashford. In 1913 she gave birth to her first child just nine days after Vivian himself was married. Elizabeth's son was named Charles, after her brother and was registered as Charles William Vincent. With the family's penchant for 'name changing', the boy eventually adopted the name 'Alan' and later signed official documents as Alan Clarke. Elizabeth was living with Ashford at 39 Spital Terrace, Gainsborough, in Lincolnshire at the time. She was now using the name Rosamund Elizabeth Clarke.

Elizabeth gave birth to a second child on May 4, 1919; a girl whom she named Enid Rosamund Lois Clarke. The birth took place at the home of her mother at Granville House, Overcliffe, Gravesend.

The 'Beth' of Vivian's novel *Ash* is clearly his sister Elizabeth. Vivian paints her as very self-centred and a social snob. In the novel 'Beth' is portrayed at shuddering at her grandparents' Norfolk dialect manner of speech and attempting to eradicate its appearance elsewhere in her family. It is something which actually sticks in Vivian's mind for in one of his later 'serious novels', *Other Gods* (1945) he portrays a character intriguingly called 'Rosalind' in a similar manner to 'Beth'. 'Rosalind disliked Norfolk dialect: she thought it common.'[5] Elizabeth certainly seemed a snob for not only did she elevate her father to the status of 'gentleman' but she was not satisfied with being plain Mrs Clarke, even with the 'e' on the end! She took her husband's middle name of Vincent and used it as a hyphenated surname 'Vincent-Clarke', so that when her daughter came to be married she gave her name as Enid Rosamund Lois Vincent-Clarke. Elizabeth's eccentricity is displayed in her Last Will and Testament, made on March 17, 1941, when she gives the curious instruction that: 'My age is not to be published and on the stone already erected to my husband I wish to be inscribed Rosamund Elizabeth, wife of Ashford Vincent-Clarke...' Certainly, Ashford himself had no time for such pretences, although in his Last Will and Testament of March 31, 1939, he does refer to his wife as 'Rosamund Elizabeth Clarke' rather than 'Elizabeth Rosamond Eliza Clarke' and while acknowledging his son preferred to be known as 'Alan', he clearly puts the name in quotation marks, adding Charles William Vincent Clarke. At no time does he ever hyphenate his middle Christian name to make Vincent-Clarke.'[6]

There is one other curiosity about Vivian's sister Elizabeth. To

Vivian's daughter, as we have mentioned, she was known only as 'Aunt Diana'. 'My Aunt Diana married Vincent-Clarke but I don't think she was ever a concert singer nor had any special talents. She had two or three children and I met her very occasionally but relations with her were cool.'[7] When asked if she could explain the discrepancy of name, Vivian's daughter could shed no light on the matter. 'There does seem to be a problem about names. With us it was always Diana, her son and daughter—Alan and Rosamund, her husband Vincent (never Ashford).'[8] There is one other possible speculation. 'Diana' might well have been the name under which Elizabeth appeared on stage as, indeed, 'Beth' in *Ash* uses the name 'Pearl'. The name Diana certainly appears in several Vivian books as an obviously favourite name choice for various female protagonists. But it has no connection with any Cannell family name.

In spite of the similarities between *Ash* and Vivian's own background, it must be pointed out that Vivian's daughter, Mrs Katharine Ashton, is inclined to dismiss its relevance. 'As for the likenesses in *Ash*—it was a novel, and a novelist would weave facts into his story but alter or embroider them as it suited him; and probably that was the case with *Ash*.' While this is obviously true, it is my belief that many of the facts of Vivian's unhappy childhood are mirrored in *Ash* with the emotional trauma that pursued him into adulthood. Incidents in *Ash* are demonstrably accurate when related to Vivian's early life.

Vivian was now living at Overcliffe, Gravesend, with his mother and younger sister Olive. If we can accept *Ash*, it was a house secured by his army gratuity and pension. But Vivian was in need of a job. Having published his first novel, he decided to go to London and look for a job in journalism.

He told his daughter that it was W. T. Stead and his daughter Christina Stead who had given him his first job in journalism.[9] This would place Vivian as obtaining a job on the *Review of Reviews*.

William Thomas Stead (1849-1912) was a famous campaigning journalist who had also been a most uncompromising critic of the Boer War. His pen was dipped in a passionate Nonconformist radicalism, being the son of a Congregationalist minister in Northumberland. Having become an editor of a Darlington newspaper at the astonishing early age of twenty-one, he was persuaded by John Morley, a famous Victorian Radical, to join his newspaper, *Pall Mall Gazette*, when Morley left the editorship, Stead took over and became one of the finest campaigning journalists of the Victorian era. It was George Newnes who helped finance Stead in launching *Review of Reviews* in 1890, a monthly containing snippets from other publications. When Stead broke up his partnership with Newnes, it motivated Newnes into launching his *Strand Magazine*.

Stead, while on his way to a peace conference in the United States was lost during the sinking of the famous White Star liner, RMS *Titanic*, during its maiden voyage on the night of April 14/15, 1912. Christina Stead, who was the *de facto* editor of *Review of Reviews* had not travelled with him on this trip.

Typical of the mysteries that surround Vivian and his career is the contradictory statement made in an atypical author's note to his novel *Curses Come Home* (1942). Vivian refers to Joseph Conrad's *Under Western Eyes* being published 'in the *English Review* of which I was at that time assistant editor to both Ford Madox Hueffer and, later, Austin Harrison.' *Under Western Eyes* was serialised in 1911. Therefore Vivian must have worked on the *English Review* from 1909, when Ford left the editorship, until the end of 1911. This, by its very time scale, would contradict the statement that it was the Steads who gave him his first journalistic job. To keep to a proper chronology, it seems more likely that Vivian left *The English Review* in late 1911 or early 1912 and took a job with the Steads on *Review of Reviews* shortly before Stead lost his life on the *Titanic*. In August 1914, Vivian then joined Murray Allisons' venture, the weekly *Land and Water*.

Vivian had left the army on December 31, 1908. We can assume that he was in London looking for work from January, 1909. Ford Madox Heuffer, who later became more famous as Ford Madox Ford (1873-1939), had launched *The English Review* in December, 1908. By the end of 1909 he had been forced to sell to Sir Alfred Mond (afterwards Lord Melchett) who then appointed Austin Harrison (1873–1928) as editor. Heuffer, whose mother was the daughter of the Pre-Raphaelite painter, Ford Madox Brown, had written some early novels in collaboration with Joseph Conrad but went on to be best known for his own *The Good Soldier* (1915) and the tetralogy *Parade's End*, (1924–1928). When the monarchy changed their name from Saxe-Coburg Gotha to Windsor in 1917 because of anti-German feeling, they advised all others with German names to do likewise. Heuffer then made the change to Ford. Ford Madox Ford is regarded as one of the great literary editors but more for his work on the *Transatlantic Review* than the *English Review*.

According to Ford's biographer it was Arthur Marwood who suggested the idea of the new literary magazine and Joseph Conrad who named it. Gerald Duckworth became its publisher and its editorial offices were in Ford's own flat at 84 Holland Park Avenue. In the summer of 1908, as the idea of the publication progressed, Ford took on Douglas Goldring as a young editorial assistant. 'What he wanted was a youth who was experienced in proof correction, and willing to undertake all the sub-editorial tasks without expecting to contribute'.[10] Goldring was then working for Ford's friend P. Anderson Graham, editor of *Country Life*.

The first issue of *English Review*, dated December, 1908, the very month Vivian left the army, was a bulky affair in blue paper covers. Its contributors are now legend. Thomas Hardy, Henry James, Joseph Conrad, John Galsworthy, Leo Tolstoy, and H.G. Wells. There was no doubt that Ford was an extravagant spender; by May he confessed to Arnold Bennett that he was losing £300 a month on the magazine.

For Vivian, son of a farm labourer and an ex-private soldier with no formal schooling outside of the parochial system and Army, to be offered a job on the *English Review* was, in the social context of the time, rather surprising. Had the young man already lost his East Anglian rural accent which so distressed 'Beth' in *Ash* and 'Rosalind' in *Other Gods* (1945)? Perhaps. Now here he was, aged twenty-six, plunged into the ambience of the literary elite of the country, scions of public schools and universities. Ford had published his first novel *The Shifting of Fire* in 1892, when he was only nineteen, and, in hiring Vivian, perhaps he had sympathy for the gauche young ex-soldier, who had produced his first novel at the age of twenty-four.

Vivian's job was to help out Goldring, who was only working part-time on the journal 'in the evenings, after leaving *Country Life*'.[11] The job was correcting and reading proofs and preparing the publication for the printers. It is unlikely that Vivian was ever 'assistant editor', as he claimed, but rather an editorial assistant. By June 1909, the *English Review* had run into deep financial difficulties. A coolness had risen between Ford and Conrad, who had been close friends, over the magazine. Indeed, not only was Ford in trouble with his business life but his wife Elsie had moved out of the flat and was suing for divorce. In Ford's Holland Park Avenue flat, which served as the editorial offices, Ford was openly living with a young German-Jewish girl, much to the scandalised embarrassment of his friends. The divorce case came up on January 11, 1910, and the *decree nisi* would have become automatic except that Elsie Hueffer was told that her daughters, being Catholics, would suffer grave injury if their parents were divorced. She abandoned her suit.[12]

But Ford's other troubles would not evaporate. By the end of 1909 the magazine was bankrupt in fact if not in law. Ford's close friend, the author Violet Hunt [1866-1942], persuaded Sir Alfred Mond, afterwards Lord Melchett, to take an interest in the publication. Sir Alfred was involved with the publishers Chapman and Hall. He bought out Duckworth for a 'derisory' sum[13] and immediately appointed Austin Harrison, a former *Daily Mail* journalist, as editor. It was with the thirteenth issue, December 1909, the last issue which Ford presided over with full editorial control, that Duckworth's imprint was replaced by Chapman & Hall. Goldring also left the journal with that issue and was replaced by Norman Douglas. (George) Norman Douglas (1868-1952) was about to publish his first book *Siren Land* (1911). He went on to establish himself as both a novelist and talented travel writer, best known for his novel *South Wind* (1917).

As for Ford, Goldring remarked:
'But by the beginning of 1910 Ford had not only lost his review. His marriage had collapsed, he was completely penniless, some of his closest friends had deserted him and he was in deadly fear that the affections of his daughters would eventually be alienated. Moreover his always highly sensitized nervous system was again giving way under the strain which was constant anxiety, disappointment and a bitter feeling of injustice had put upon it.'[14]

It is hard to see where the young ex-soldier, Vivian, figured in these machinations. Certainly, according to Vivian, he survived the change and continued to serve as an editorial dogsbody to Norman Douglas, reading proofs and generally learning the journalist's trade. The offices were now at 3 Henrietta Street, by London's Covent Garden.

The English Review was no mean place to start a career in literary journalism. In spite of its early financial difficulties under Ford Madox Ford, it lasted until July 1937. Apart from the literary luminaries already mentioned, its columns saw the first published verses of D.H. Lawrence, Frederic Manning and Wyndham Lewis. *The English Review* was as good as a university education for an aspiring writer such as Vivian. 'No doubt Ford gave his successor every assistance while the change-over was taking place, and Norman Douglas...helped maintain the continuity of literary standard which Ford had established.'[15] One thing Ford had insisted on: 'The first thing the novelist has to learn is self-effacement—that first, and that always.'[16] Vivian became self-effacing to a fault.

Ford had firm views on the craft of fiction writing and, particularly the novel form. He hated any misuse of English. He warned writers to avoid 'being clever'.

'I should say myself that the art of writing in English received the numbing blow of a sandbag when Rosetti wrote, at the age of eighteen *The Blessed Damozel*. From that time forward and until today—and for how many years to come!—the idea has been inherent in the mind of the English writer that writing was a matter of digging for obsolete words with which to express ideas forever dead and gone. Stevenson did this, of course, as carefully as any Pre-Raphaelite, though instead of going to medieval books he ransacked the seventeenth century.'[17]

Vivian seemed to learn his lessons well. During the early part of 1909 he was hard at work on his second novel. The novel, *The Woman Tempted Me*, was semi-autobiographical, starting out in Norfolk, featuring a young man arguing with his father about his future career, running away and joining a cavalry regiment in the same manner that Vivian had—under an assumed name 'Roy Henry Vane', which seems to echo 'Evelyn Henry Vivian'. This protagonist, Vane, becomes, like Vivian, a lance-corporal. But Vane falls in love with the wife of his sergeant, a girl called Marjorie Hayes. He deserts the army and they elope to South America. Vane winds up selling guns to the Boers during the South African War and separates from Marjorie. When he eventually returns to England he learns of her death.

Vivian did not take his 'moral tale', which he subtitled 'the story of a selfish man', to Gay & Bird, who had published his first novel. Perhaps he was advised by Harrison or Douglas to find a publisher who could cope better in presenting 'serious' fiction'. He went to Andrew Melrose, a popular London publisher, who issued it in a 6s edition in September of that year. It does not appear to have been noticed by any major critics although Melrose also reissued it in a 1s popular edition in May, 1912. Undeterred by this lack of interest, Vivian went to work on a third novel.

The salary for an editorial assistant on the *English Review* was not over generous. One can imagine Vivian struggling to keep the Gravesend home together and finding it a tough job as he is beset by increasing bills. It was a problem faced by another Charles Vivian who was also lamenting the tough times in verse:

> The price of food, of coal, of clothes,
>   Is daily getting more,
> While tax-collectors and the like
>   For ever haunt my door.

But though this universal rise
Fills me with fear and rage,
One thing for ever keeps the same—
My meagre weekly wage![18]

The 'other Mr Vivian' (1884–1966) was also a journalist who had become assistant editor of *Pearson's Magazine* in 1910. He was to have a distinguished career in journalism, served in France with the Royal Artillery and then became editor of *Novel Magazine* then *Cassell's Magazine* from 1922-24. It would seem, therefore, both Vivian's paths should have crossed. After writing some books, such as *Fun With Science, Things to Make and Do,* and *Heard This One?* Charles Vivian went into public relations as press officer for the British Empire Exhibition, then the Royal Empire Society before taking his wife and sons to Bermuda around 1939/1940 where he worked in postal censorship during the war years. There was an interview with him about his career in *The Bermudian* in 1944. He returned to England in 1947. His death notice in *The Times*, mentions a Requiem Mass was given for him at Catholic Church in Painswick, in Gloucestershire on January 20, 1966. Bibliographers, including myself, were misled for some time into ascribing his verse and ballads to E. Charles Vivian. However, as early as 1933, as we shall examine later, Charles Vivian felt it necessary to publicly differentiate himself from his fiction-writing namesake.

The third novel was to be another tragic love story with an East Anglian setting. Its heroine, perhaps as a genuflection to his editor, Austin Harrison, was called Violet Harrison. Andrew Melrose published it in September 1910. This time *The English Review* felt obliged to publish a notice of the novel by their young editorial assistant. Perhaps Harrison even wrote it himself, trying not to be too harsh on his young employee.

'What Lord Rosebery said mournfully about Carnegie's Libraries the other day applies to this novel and its author. Talent, observation, facility of expression, a genuine story—telling vein—all this, but all, shall we say, commercially used, applied, that is, to turn out a successful book quickly rather than to render life faithfully or reveal character. Just the opposite to Ibsen or Arnold Bennett. Yet it is a very readable tale, swift and flowing. It has the tracery of the Victorian dramatist, characters and situations are *voulus* [sic]. It stands for the school that Mr Ford Madox Hueffer does not stand for. That is why the judgment of *The English Review* is somewhat severe.[19]

Like the good professional that he was rapidly becoming, Vivian set to work on his fourth novel, *Following Feet*. Again, it was published by Melrose in February 1911. Once more he set it in East Anglia with a hero returned from the wars having served, significantly, in 'C' Squadron of 'the glorious Fifth'. It is a tough love story with fascinating cross currents of ideas and themes found later in *Ash*. The hero, having returned home, finds his sister has been seduced. He kills the seducer without hesitation or a tremor of remorse. Then he finds that his victim was the brother of the girl he loves.

This time *The English Review* was more enthusiastic.

'We can recommend this novel to all who are looking for dramatic and thrilling story... A book full of quick actions and thought, compressing a vital story to the convenient dimension of a dramatic few thousand words, with vividness of action and of cleverly drawn character.'[20]

Towards the end of his career, Vivian decided to return to the theme of this novel which had a passing resemblance to Conrad's *Under Western Eyes*, curiously serialised in *The English Review* at the time Vivian's book was published. In Conrad's novel, set in nineteenth century Russia, Razumov betrays his fellow student Haldin to the secret police and certain death. Sent to Geneva as a government spy, Razumov then falls in love with Haldin's sister. Vivian decided to rewrite *Following Feet* as *Curses Come Home*. His choice of title made it sound like a typical Vivian thriller and he does introduce one of his favourite detectives, Detective Inspector Terence Byrne of Scotland Yard, into the early part of the story, setting it up more as mystery tale before Byrne gracefully withdraws leaving the 'serious romance' to take place.

In an author's note Vivian explains:

'The theme of this novel is one that I attempted to develop in a crude and immature work which was published before I saw the serialisation or even the script of Joseph Conrad's *Under Western Eyes* when that was published in the *English Review*, of which I was at the time assistant editor under both Ford Madox Hueffer and, later, Austin Harrison. I make this statement to save myself from a possible charge of plagiarism. The only plagiarism of which I am guilty is that of a badly constructed piece of my own work, which has been out of print for some years, and which I wish never to see resuscitate.'[21]

Even with this warning the critic of the *Times Literary Supplement* was wont to bemoan the book was not a mystery story.

'Detective stories fix a frame of mind unlike any other. After conforming to this with chapters one and three of *Curses Come Home*, Mr Vivian breaks away from it. The murder, the detective, and Scotland Yard are to serve as an excuse for a passionate love story. Perhaps this could be done; it all depends on the way interest is transferred from one subject to the other. When the reader keeps asking himself "what has all this to do with the murder?" the author has failed, and this is what happens when Mr Vivian pushes Inspector Head out of his pages. And people who hanker after a passionate love story are not likely to get as far as the chapter where this one begins at last.'[22]

Obviously the critic touched a raw nerve and in an atypical response Vivian wrote to the *Times Literary Supplement* pointing out that *Curses Come Home* was a serious novel and not a mystery story.[23] Yet in fairness to the *Times Literary Supplement*, Vivian had brought the criticism on himself with his choice of title and the introduction of the character of Inspector Terence Byrne. It was as if Sherlock Holmes had suddenly appeared in *The White Company*.

Melrose had now published three books by Vivian, but none of them had sold to America as his first novel had done, nor did any, except *The Woman Tempted Me*, go to reprints. Vivian looked for a new publisher.

His next novel, *Passion Fruit*, was an extraordinarily tough tale. Again there is the inevitable theme of the protagonist Gerald Lathom being the son of a bad marriage. He falls in love with Isabel but she rejects him for one Cecil Ashburton. 'A rotter, a drunken rotter with a habit of neglecting his wife for other women.' Gerald and Isabel's paths cross again in Lucknow, India, which Vivian, from his personal experience there, is able to paint very vividly. Isabel, now known as Belle, is a widow and having an affair with a man named Verrinder. Verrinder suddenly commits suicide. The person who discovers his body says: 'There was a curious brown-edged, whitish sort of patch on his forehead—like nothing I'd ever seen before.'

Then Gerald's friend Stevens arrives in Lucknow, meets Belle and falls in love with her. Stevens eventually returns to England and marries his fiancée, Jessie Conway. But when he hears Belle is in trouble, he deserts her and goes back to Lucknow. In the meantime we find that Belle has developed 'an acute case of anæsthetic leprosy developing very rapidly'. She has picked this up from her former lover Verrinder. We are obviously dealing with euphemisms for contagious sexual diseases. Leprosy was sufficiently horrendous in the minds of the public in those days to stand for the unmentionable forms of venereal diseases. Belle sends for Gerald and he sees in the now tragic, hard-faced woman, a glimpse of the young girl he had once fallen in love with and, if the truth were known, still loves. It is, however, to be a farewell meeting. When he is gone she prepares some poison and takes it. When she is found, in the morning, her face is not peaceful, the terror of what was facing her is mirrored there.

Stevens then arrives. Too late.

It was not a tale for the squeamish. The *Times Literary Supplement* commented: 'A novel which shows much power in dealing with a personal destiny savaged by love, over-mastered by passion.'[24]

Vivian took *Passion Fruit* to William Heinemann who published it in a 5s edition in March, 1912. Heinemann had earned a reputation as a publisher who was prepared to take risks, even with books that others felt were morally improper. Conversely, he had rejected other titles on moral grounds including August Strindberg's work. Among others whose early work he rejected were James Joyce, Edgar Wallace, Gertrude Stein, P. C. Wren and Compton Mackenzie. In John St. John's official history of the house of Heinemann, there is an intriguing reference.

'... like his competitors he could never afford to forget the censorship exercised not only by the libraries but also by the authorities. There was the threatening example of *Passion Fruit* (1912) by Charles E. Vivian [sic]. After the court had pronounced it obscene the police came round to Bedford Street and burned the remaining stock on the office stove.'[25]

Unfortunately John St. John died in 1990 when his book was published and examination of his research material lodged with Octopus, who now own Heinemann, has failed to come up with his source for this statement.[26] Records of Bow Street magistrates, the nearest court to the publishers, show no cases involving *Passion Fruit*. Similarly, an examination of selective publishing magazines of the day has failed to turn up corroborating evidence. Because of the way the censorship laws worked in England, what was banned by one magistrate's court could be approved of under the jurisdiction of a neighbouring court, the lack of evidence does not mean to say that St. John was in error. However, later books of Vivian do bear the legend 'by the author of *Passion Fruit*' which could indicate that the book was not universally banned. Conversely, it has been argued, that the publishers might have been attempting to 'cash-in' on the notoriety of the publication. It is, sadly, yet another infuriating mystery that may never be solved. *Passion Fruit* remained the one and only book of Vivian's that Heinemann published and, perhaps, that is enough circumstantial evidence to support the statement of the historian of William Heinemann.

Clearly, something did happen to stay Vivian's career as a novelist in 1912. He was not to produce another novel until 1914 and then it would be published by Holden & Hardingham. He only published one more novel in 1915 and then wrote no more until 1923. It was only then that he was to find a regular supportive publisher for his novels.

It would appear that by the time of the Heinemann publication, Vivian had left *The English Review* and joined the Steads on *Review of Reviews*, which Stead had launched on January 15, 1890. Vivian had joined *Review of Reviews* at a time when Stead had just returned from one of his anti-war crusading visits to Constantinople. On March 17, 1912, Fred B. Smith, organiser of The National Men and Religious Forward Movement, telegraphed Stead inviting him to address a meeting in Carnegie Hall with President Taft, British Ambassador James (afterwards Lord) Bryce and others on April 21. One of Stead's last articles in the April, 1912, *Review of Reviews* was about this World Peace conference. He added: 'I expect to leave by the *Titanic* on April 10, and hope I shall be back in London in May.'[27]

Estelle Stead says her father took his family from Cambridge House, Wimbledon Park, down to his country house at Holly Bush, Hayling Island and spent his last Sunday at home there. He was full of enthusiasm and delight at going on the maiden voyage of the *Titanic*. He stood on the deck waving to his wife as the great ship steamed off on its first and last voyage.[28]

The tragic death of Stead in the *Titanic* disaster had happened at the same time of the publication of *Passion Fruit*. Because of the system of lack of initials or signatures in *Review of Reviews* none of Vivian's work for the publication can now be traced.

His first known short story 'How the Girl Came to Bentley's' was published in *Nash's Magazine*, in April, 1910. At the going rate for new writers at this time, the story would probably have netted Vivian three guineas (£3 3s.).

The year 1912 was to yield two other major events of significance in Vivian's life. Firstly, he was discharged from the Army Reserve as being medically unfit for further service from February 7, 1912.[29] The other event was he had met Marion Christmas Harvie, the daughter of a solicitor based at Serjeant's Inn, London, and they had fallen in love. Vivian was now thirty years old and Marion was six years his senior. It could be said that Vivian had now completed his journeyman's apprenticeship and come to the gateway of a new section of his life.

Notes

1. From information contained in Birth, Marriage, Death Certificates, St Catherine's House, London.
2. *Ash*, as above, pp. 225/226.
3. *Ibid.*, p 227.
4. Death certificate.
5. *Other Gods* (1945), p. 283.
6. Wills at Somerset House.
7. Mrs Katharine Ashton to author, February 14, 1993.
8. Mrs Katharine Ashton to author, January 28, 1994.
9. Mrs Katharine Ashton to author, April 23, 1990.
10. *The Last Pre-Raphaelite: A Record of the Life and Writings of Ford Madox Ford*, Douglas Goldring, Macdonald & Co, London, 1948. p. 140.
11. *Ibid.*
12. *The Last Pre-Raphaelite*, as above, p. 153/160.
13. *The Last Pre-Raphaelite*, as above, p. 151.
14. *The Last Pre-Raphaelite*, as above, p. 152.
15. *Ibid.*
16. *The Good Soldier*, Ford Madox Ford, Mayflower-Dell, London, edition, July, 1965. (Table-talk appendix, p. 254).
17. *Ibid.* p. 252.
18. *The Red Magazine*, March, 1909.
19. *The English Review*, November, 1910.
20. *The English Review*, May, 1911.
21. *Curses Come Home* (1942), p-vii..
22. *Times Literary Supplement*, May 23, 1942.
23. *Times Literary Supplement*, June 6, 1942.
24. *Times Literary Supplement*, March 21, 1912.
25. *William Heinemann*. John St John, Heinemann, London, 1990. p. 46/47.
26. Mrs Jean Rose ALA, Deputy Group Library, Octopus Publishing Group Library, letter to author, August 20, 1991.
27. *Review of Reviews*, April, 1912.
28. *The Life of W.T. Stead*, Frederic White, Jonathan Cape, London, 1925, p.

310/313. See also *Crusader in Babylon: W. T. Stead and the Pall Mall Gazette*. Raymond L. Schults, University of Nebraska Press, Lincoln, Nebraska, USA, 1972. p. 251.

[29.] Public Record Office, WO 97/6137 XC 197528.

CHAPTER FOUR

EDITORSHIP

It seems that with the success in placing a short story in *Nash's Magazine* Vivian was turning to short fiction and had been able to place some boys' adventure stories, set in Africa, with the highly prestigious *Boy's Own Paper*. *Boy's Own* had been launched by the Religious Tract Society on January 18, 1879. The popularity of the publication was demonstrated by the fact that within four years it had reached a circulation of a quarter of a million. But the Religious Tract Society was considered too forbidding a body to be named as publishers and so the fronting organisation was soon named 'Leisure Hour'. *Boy's Own*'s first editor, the redoubtable G. A. Hutchison, was still in office when Vivian began to sell his short stories to the journal. Hutchison had a talent for spotting good writers before they achieved fame. In the pages of his magazine appeared the fiction of W. H. G. Kingston, Jules Verne, Talbot Baines Reed and R. M. Ballantine. When Hutchison retired later in 1913 another remarkable editor took over—G. J. H. Northcroft, whose *Writing for Children* (A. & C. Black, 1935) became a classic of the 'do's and don'ts' of children's writing.[1]

Vivian was to have a long association with *Boys' Own Paper* writing not only short stories but exciting adventure serials such as 'Aztec Gold'[2] and 'A Scout of the '45'. *Boys' Own Paper* actually published this as a novel under its own imprint as a hardcover edition the following year, 1923. This was an adventure tale set against the

Jacobite uprising with its hero, twenty-year-old Arthur England running away from the dictatorial guardianship of his uncle to become a soldier. Vivian, it seems, was unable to escape from his own background even in his boy's fiction. Arthur joins forces with a blacksmith's son, Tom Parker, and they rescue the heroine, Dorothy Trafford, who has been kidnapped. The book was illustrated by G. Browne. It was a successful publication and reprinted several times. The *Times Literary Supplement* noted: 'a good specimen of its kind, well written and containing a number of picturesque figures.'[3]

When he became a Ward Lock author, Vivian was to return to boy's adventure fiction twice more. In 1927 he retold the tales of *Robin Hood and His Merry Men*, published in the company's Sunshine Series. This was to become, without a doubt, his most reprinted book, with regular editions from 1927 through to October 1950, three years after his death. He wrote the book while living in Paris.

Perhaps it was being in Paris, away from England, that caused Vivian to turn back to those very English legends of the Sherwood Forest outlaw. He retold the whole saga from the time of Robin being made an outlaw until his death by treachery. It was illustrated with thirty colour plates by Harry George Theaker. Theaker (1873–1954) was one of the most popular illustrators of the day although one critic said: 'His children's book illustrations tended to be banal and uninspired but were often pleasantly coloured.' He illustrated editions of *Gulliver's Travels*, *Don Quixote*, *The Water Babies* and *Grimm Fairy Tales*. The *Times Literary Supplement* felt that Vivian's retelling 'has retained much of the story's charm and freshness'.[4] Six years later, after a new edition was issued, the *Times Literary Supplement* confirmed its original opinion.[5] This was a successful book for Vivian.

Vivian's last foray into boy's adventure fiction was a novel about young Richard Dangerham, yeoman and servant to Edward, the Black Prince. *The Black Prince* was published in August 1936, as No 19 in Ward Lock's Sentinel Series. *Robin Hood*, after going through seven editions in the Sunshine Series, had also just been re-launched in a new Sentinel Series edition. *The Black Prince* was illustrated with a colour frontispiece by J. F. Campbell. It was a well-crafted adventure with plenty of feats of derring-do. As the publisher's publicity assured readers: 'We may be sure that in the experienced hands of E. Charles Vivian, the story of young Richard Dangerham . . . loses nothing in the telling.'

In their study, *The Men Behind Boys' Fiction*, Lofts and Adley state that Vivian also, during his early writing career, contributed boys' adventure stories to *Young England*. A closer examination of these stories, written between 1905 and 1909, shows the author to be an Edward Vivian. While the stories deal with many of the subjects which were to fascinate Vivian later in his career, I do not believe that these are early examples of his work. His first book was issued under the name 'Evelyn C. H. Vivian'. There is nothing to support the idea that he also used the pseudonym 'Edward Vivian'.

On September 3 1913, Vivian married Marion Christmas Harvie. The marriage took place at the parish church of Heene, now a part of Worthing in Sussex. Marion's father, Edgar Christmas Harvie had recently died. He had been a solicitor in London with a practise at 8 Serjeant's Inn, London EC4, and it was in London that Vivian had met her. Vivian's sister Olive Cannell went to Heene with him to be one of his witnesses. The other witnesses were Marion's mother, Caroline Mary Harvie, and Marion's sister, Elizabeth Adams Harvie. Vivian now gave his name as 'Charles Henry Vivian otherwise Cannell'.

In his article in *Armchair Detective*, W. O. G. Lofts wrote: 'In 1913, at Worthing in Sussex, he married Marion Christmas Harvie, the daughter of a wealthy family.'[6] Vivian's daughter claims that this is an incorrect statement: 'Mr Lofts came to see me some years ago. He informed me that my mother was 'a rich woman'. This, of course, was far from true: she came from an ordinary professional family, with the same sort of means as their counterparts today. But Mr Lofts would not accept this, and repeated that "yes, your mother was a rich woman".'[7]

Another minor mystery emerges for, on his marriage certificate,

Vivian gives his address as Gravesend. Yet on the same day as his wedding, September 3 1913, Vivian signed a Will and there gave his address as 22 Abingdon Mansions, Kensington. The Will was simple and remained his only Will, enacted on his death in 1947. It left all his property to his wife and appointed her sole executrix. The two witnesses were H. Edward Harvie, Marion's brother, of 8 Serjeant's Inn, London EC4, and Marion's mother, Caroline Mary Harvie of Norfolk Lodge, West Worthing. Edward Harvie was killed during the 1914–18 War.

The explanation to these two different addresses, given on the same day, may be that Vivian thought of Gravesend as his home but had a *pied-a-terre* in Abingdon Mansions to be closer to his work. Whether Vivian and his bride lived in Abingdon Mansions, Kensington, for a while, it is not certain. Certainly within a few years, they had moved into Orchard Cottage, St John's Road, Orpington.

According to Katharine Vivian, her mother 'was devoted to my father and gave him every kind of support. She had no occupation apart from charitable work'.

Vivian now had a commission to write his first non-fiction work, a guidebook to Peru, part of Pitman's South American Handbook series. It has been suggested that Vivian used this opportunity to take Marion on 'honeymoon' to Peru in order to research the book. Unfortunately, Vivian's daughter cannot throw any light on this. 'If my father ever went to South America, it would have been before I was born and I do not remember hearing about it.'[8]

The guidebook, simply called *Peru*, was published in July 1914, a work of 235 pages, with 2 colour maps and 15 photographic plates. An American edition was sold to the D. Appleton Co, of New York, who published it concurrently. The American magazine *Outlook*, reviewing the book, welcomed it warmly. 'Mr Vivian's book will serve a good purpose if it further helps us to understand that Peru is of surpassing interest historically and economically.'[9] It is the *Wisconsin Library Bulletin* which gives weight to the contention that Vivian did not go to Peru but might simply have been a product of a competent journalist, worked up from documents available in London.

'The descriptions are based to a large extent on public documents and are far from giving an adequate presentation of conditions as they actually exist. On the other hand, there is a concreteness in the information concerning imports and exports, populations, water supply, streets, transportation systems, harbour, tonnage etc. which places the volume far above the average books on South American countries.'[10]

The New York Times Review of Books, the literary section of the newspaper, indicated Vivian's concentration on mercantile facts rather than geographic description.

'Peru also is an excellent field for the expenditure of sagacious American effort. It offers opportunities of great importance and of many kinds for men who care to invest in the country and help in its development, and it has a large and growing capacity for foreign wares and merchandise. Mr Vivian, in his book, sets forth information that will be helpful to Americans who come into the way of considering whether they care to take shares in Peruvian companies.'[11]

Certainly, Vivian's *Peru* became a standard text for a while and he was later to use a South American background in several subsequent novels.

With *Peru* out of the way, Vivian returned to writing a 'serious' novel. The title was *Divided Ways* and concerned Alan Hope of Hope Brothers, merchants in Africa, who returns to a new life in London with his wife, Nina, pure, gentle and caring. But he meets Mary North, a former girl-friend, strong, materialist and discerning, a proto 'Beth' character. Mary North is a self-centred character while Nina, the wife, has a touching, moral dignity and self-control.

Alan and Mary begin an affair which then ends unhappily and Hope is left with his marriage in ruins, living in the same house as his wife but separately. Vivian now had to find another publisher and placed the book with Holden & Hardingham who published it in November, 1914. The *Times Literary Supplement* was somewhat scathing. '*Divided Ways* by E. Charles Vivian is one among many modern novels infused with a certain kind of sentimental feminism'. But the critic did concede that 'Stripped of emotional trappings, the story of *Divided Ways*, which is worked out with a good deal of skill, has one or two very moving scenes . . .'[12]

There was a more sympathetic review in *Colour*[13] a monthly arts orientated magazine which had been launched in August, 1914, and to which Vivian had, with its first issue, started to contribute short stories. He was to appear fairly regularly in *Colour* until 1923.

As Europe prepared for war, Vivian was able to secure another commission from J. E. Hodder Williams of the publishers Hodder and Stoughton. This time it was an ambitious study of the British Army. *The British Army from Within, by one who has served in it* (the author's name, E. Charles Vivian, appears on the title page) was to be part of Hodder and Stoughton's 'The Army from Within Series', catering for the new interest in the military manoeuvrings in the pre-war lull. Vivian relies heavily on his experiences in South Africa to lend colour to the work. By the time it appeared in October, what was to become 'The Great War of 1914–18' had already commenced. *Review of Reviews* gave a sympathetic notice saying the book 'gives much enlightenment.'[14] *Land and Water* felt that it 'will make very instructive reading not only to all those who have enlisted or are about to enlist, but to all those interested—and at the present moment who is not?—in the welfare of the British Army'.[15] It sold very well running to four different editions by December, 1915. It also sold to an interested America where George H. Doran of New York published it. 'It is written with apparent fullness of knowledge and with an evidently sincere desire to convey information', observed *Nation,*[16] while the US *Review of Reviews* felt 'The book is an answer to many questions that have arisen since the great war began.[17]

The New York Times Review of Books, however, encapsulated some of Vivian's criticism of the army of 1914 which, by Christmas and the onset of 'trench warfare' was shown to have been valid.

'Mr Vivian, in his book on the British Army, points out that this body is now undergoing a revolution, and that many of the ideas will have to be discarded which have prevailed in the past about the small army which has been doing Great Britain's fighting in the four quarters of the world. 'The new army', he terms the vast force now being called to the colors, and he points out that this new army, quite unlike the old British Army, 'is not a thing apart from the nation: it is the nation'.

'Rapidity in training the legions of recruits is the great necessity which England now faces, and in commenting on this fact the author casts some slight doubt on the value in all practical respects for field service of the training which the young soldiers are getting from the veteran non-commissioned officers of other days, who past the fighting age themselves, are being called out in large numbers of train squads of recruits. Mr Vivian points out as a 'minor drawback' the fact that these old soldiers are out of touch with some of the details of modern weapons and drill. The field gun, for instance, now in use by the British, was only introduced after the Boer War.

'"It is essential that the new army should begin training itself at the earliest possible moment," says the author, and for this reason "there are endless opportunities for the man with brains who enlists at the present time." No man can foresee, of course, how large the new army will be on a peace footing after this war is over, but "not while a first-class power remains on the Continent of Europe will conscription cease altogether," although the war will probably result in the end of universal conscription; in any event, a considerable portion of the new British Army will have to be retained.'[18]

In this prediction, Vivian was proved correct and it was not until the late 1950s that 'conscription' was finally ended.

Hodder and Stoughton were, like many another publishers, producing war related books to boost morale. Indeed, the Government encouraged it and the Rt. Hon Charles Gurney Masterman (1873–1927), former Chancellor of the Duchy of Lancaster, had been appointed director of Wellington House (Propaganda Department), a post he retained from 1914 to 1918, attracting a group of twenty to thirty writers who were engaged on war propaganda work. He encouraged writers like Edgar Wallace, the prolific William Le Queux, whose books numbered 209, and others to write war related books. Wallace was producing a weekly part work *War of the Nations* for George Newnes. Le Queux had written the first issues but

Wallace took over, producing this illustrated account of the war, and reaching 155 issues. It was also issued in ten separate volumes. It has no pretensions to be history but was simply a morale boosting exercise. Wallace, as usual, was rather prolific in this field turning out several other works such as *Famous Scottish Regiments* (1914), *Field Marshal Sir John French* (1914), *Heroes All: Gallant Deeds of the War* (1914), *Standard History of the War* (1914), and *Kitchener's Army* (1915).[19]

Vivian now entered into the same feverish activity for a while. He continued to write for Hodder and Stoughton, who were publishing a series of *Daily Telegraph* War Books and an 'At the Front Series'. Vivian was asked to write *With the Royal Army Medical Corps at the Front*, published at the end of 1914, and *With the Scottish Regiments at the Front*, dated 1914 but not published until January, 1915. They were competent journalistic jobs. *Land and Water* observed of the former title that it 'contains some exceptionally interesting chapters compiled from the actual experiences of men of the medical service now at the front'.[20]

J. E. Hodder Williams was himself interested in the activities of the Red Cross and asked Vivian to write a joint work with him, Vivian's name going as first author on the title page, on the organisation.[21] *The Way of the Red Cross*, printed for *The Times* by Hodder and Stoughton, had a preface by Queen Alexandra with all profits going to *The Times* Fund for the Sick and Wounded. Vivian had to travel to hospitals catering for the war wounded to interview soldiers, nurses and doctors for the book. He shows a perceptive eye for story and personalities. It appeared in March and was reprinted in July. In American, George H. Doran produced a US edition.

The New York Times Review of Books gave a lengthy notice to it, stating that 'the authors have gathered many dramatic and touching stories from the wounded, and these furnish the most interesting chapters'. One thing that Vivian had picked up on, and this was early in 1915, at a time when the British Army refused to acknowledge the existence of the phenomenon, was 'shell shock'. Vivian's word for it, before 'shell shock' became accepted, was 'shellitis'. Today it is called

Post Traumatic Stress Disorder. 'Victims, though not wounded, lost all interest in life... The nurses find that shattered nerves are much harder to cure than broken bones.' The reviewer observed: 'This book is a good one for those in quest of details about Red Cross methods, incidentally it shows how little romance and how much unpleasant work falls to the lot of the nurses.'[22]

The *Boston Transcript* was even more enthusiastic.

'While an excellent survey is made of the technical organisation of the Red Cross among the Allies, the authors have jewelled their story with countless cameos of life as Red Cross workers see it, poignant dramas of manhood and womanhood, touches of humour, of tears, of splendid sacrifice and uncomplaining courage of the soul.'[23]

Clearly these books demonstrated Vivian had become a competent journalist. However, he still felt the need to obtain recognition as a serious novelist and once more he returned to the theme that seemed to haunt him—a young man's conflict with his father. He began work on another novel and entitled it *The Young Man Absalom*.

He set the story in a manufacturing town. Philip Crayford is the owner of a machine making plant, an autocratic ironmaster. His son Paul, returning home from Cambridge, takes his place in management but comes into conflict with the way his father is ruling his workforce. He joins the workers in a strike which leads to his fiancée breaking off the engagement because of Paul's commitment to socialism. His path leads to his death in a car crash and causes his father to concede to his worker's demands.

There is a subsidiary recurring theme here; not only the conflict between father and son, which Vivian had experienced, but death of the son resulting in the father realising the error of his ways and making amends. In the short story 'The Yellow Streak,' published in pamphlet form in 1921, Henry Hudson is abused by his father for being a coward. He is sent to South Africa where the boy is killed saving his companions and the father is devastated. One wonders whether we are witnessing a fantasy of Vivian, that one day he would be able to make his father perform an act of apology and reconciliation for the miserable childhood he had endured.

Once more Vivian had to find a new publisher and this time Chapman and Hall, erstwhile publishers of *The English Review*, issued the book in January, 1915, in a six shilling edition. There was a sale to America where E. P. Dutton off New York published it in July of the same year.

While *Colour*[24] gave its usual friendly review, the *Times Literary Supplement*, felt that 'E. Charles Vivian has not been quite judicious in choosing a title for his new novel *The Young Man Absalom*. It inevitably suggests that the story was written to fit the title, and it keeps in the background of the reader's mind the tragedy of David and his son, which one tries to rewrite at one's peril'.[25] The critic felt that 'a chief merit of the story is its sincerity... Mr Vivian has shown, certainly, that he can handle a plot with no little dexterity, keeping for his climax that dash through the night by Paul in his motor car which is so well described in the penultimate chapter'. *Land and Water* commented: 'Taken altogether there are many types here worth considering and we commend this book as a thoughtful and really interesting work.'[26]

In America, the *Independent* felt 'E. Charles Vivian has fused a good story and a lucid clear cut statement of the struggle of labor and capital and colored it all with intensity of sympathy and conviction'.[27]

The New York Times Review of Books section gave a very lengthy and sympathetic review.

'In one respect this story, which depicts life in an English manufacturing town, differs much from the usual English novel. For it is concerned less with that intimated and detailed portrayal of character which forms so large a part of most of the story books made in the British Isles than it is with the story it has to tell, and with, by means of the story, the things the author wishes to say about some of the immediate problems of life in England and elsewhere. The book evidently was written before the war, but the problem with which it deals has projected itself more persistently and more poignantly into the life of that nation than it ever had done before—the problem of the working man and the reciprocal relations between him and the rest of his fellow countrymen.'

The reviewer felt:

'The book tells the story, with a good deal of incident, very little plot complication and considerable apparent knowledge of conditions and points of view among English countrymen and their families, of how he [the hero] tried to bring about betterment and of the class war into which the village flames in consequence.

'Perhaps the most interesting feature is the reflection of that phase of class feeling indulged in by the industrial aristocracy towards the workers, apparently more self-conscious and consequently more intense than that of the landed gentry. The author nowhere indulges in analysis or psychology concerning this curious manifestation. He simply presents it in his characters and from their words and deeds one gathers that the basis of it is not so much conviction of God-made superiority as fear lest if so much as an inch be conceded the barbarians will rise up and overflow the land.'[28]

The reviewer observed that the book had a message for American capitalists. 'Give a man his just daily wage and he'll manage his own social regeneration'[26] The idea was echoed by the *Athenæum* which stated that: 'The novel may start more than one general reader on investigation as to how the greater number of his fellows live—a more useful purpose than the attracting of social experts.'[29] But it was, all in all, the comment of *Nation* which seemed to hit Vivian the most: 'It is all pretty trite in manner and in management not sufficiently fresh to conceal that triteness.'[30] Vivian was not tempted to write another novel for eight years and by the 1930s any sympathy he might have shown for working class rights and Socialism had vanished. Vivian's daughter recalled that Socialist politicians and Socialism had become his pet dislike.

It was in the summer of 1914 that a rich Australian, Murray (commonly called 'Jim') Allison, advertisement manager on *The Times* and later on the *Daily Telegraph*, and therefore, with a connection with Hodder and Stoughton, became the main financier behind a journal entitled *The Country Gentleman and Land and Water*. The journal had been launched in 1862 as *The Sporting Gazette* and went through several metamorphoses until in June, 1905, it had been renamed *The*

Country Gentleman and Land and Water. It was Allison's idea to change it from a 'Town and Country Newspaper' into a journal dealing exclusively with the war. It would be simply *Land and Water* with the first revamped issue in January, 1916. Vivian was given the job as assistant editor with the issue dated August 22, 1914. Perhaps this was by virtue of the Hodder and Stoughton's connection with the journal. With that issue Vivian began a six week by-lined series 'A Topographical Guide to the War Zone'.

But *Land and Water* has become irrevocably linked with the name of the crusading journalist Hilaire Belloc (1870–1953). We are told by Belloc's biographer, A. N. Wilson, that Allison, a neighbour of Belloc's at Rodmell, near Lewes in Sussex, visited Belloc at his home on September 9 and, after a three hour discussion, Belloc signed a contract to write a weekly article for *Land and Water* on the military situation.'[31] Fred Jane (of *Jane's Fighting Ships* etc.) was signed up to write naval articles. But it was Belloc's articles which were to push *Land and Water*'s circulation up to 100,000 copies a week by the late autumn of 1914. These articles were discussed by people in every street, railway train, club or officers' mess as the war progressed. Belloc's arrogant figure was to dominate *Land and Water*.

His exaggerated opinions were often based on inaccurate ideas and information. In October, 1914, a publication was circulated entitled *What I Know About the War* by 'Blare Hilloc'. When this publication was opened, it was discovered to be a notebook with blank pages.[32] Belloc consistently underestimated the strength of the German army and overestimated their casualties. He saw the war as a clash between Catholic civilisation and pagan barbarism. It was coincidental that he saw England as supporting Catholic civilisation[33] The *Daily Mail* of September 6, 1915, attacked Belloc's pieces in *Land and Water*, pointing to his mistakes and errors.

Vivian, as well as his editorial duties on *Land and Water* was still making regular story contributions to *Colour*. But work on the weekly *Land and Water* was obviously time-consuming although his by-line only occasionally appeared in the paper itself. He wrote on 'The Chivalry of India' in the September 18, 1915, issue, and contributed a lengthy article 'Needs of Nations' on the obligation of Britain, as one of the richest powers, to donate money to various charities. He gives a list of various charities and organisations and explains their needs in detail. He was also reviewing books, ranging from *A Thousand Years of Russian History* by Sonia E. Howe to a translation of Theophile Gautier's *Fortunio*. But his practical work in editing left little time in 1916 to contribute material or stories to other publications.

At this time Vivian was also having articles published in *The Asiatic Review*, formerly *The Asiatic Quarterly Review*, founded in January, 1886. Published by East and West Ltd., and issued eight times a year, the magazine was given to all members of the East India Association 'instituted for the independent and disinterested advocacy and promotion by all legitimate means of the public interests and welfare of the inhabitants of India generally.' The Rt. Hon. Lord Reay was president, and among the vice-presidents were Vivian's old commander-in-chief, Field Marshal Lord Roberts of Kandahar, Pretoria and Waterford. From 1914 through to 1917 Vivian contributed an occasional article and book review, reviewing among other things a translated volume of short stories, *The Eternal Husband*, by Fyodor Dostoevsky (Heinemann, 1917).

Land and Water certainly became the most popular weekly war journal, and Belloc was earning a staggering (for the time) £40 for his weekly article that often ran to 8000 words. He had also signed a contract with Thomas Nelson Ltd to publish these *Land and Water* articles in book form to be issued every three months as *A General History of the War*. Belloc was, if anything, egocentric. By March, 1916, he was becoming critical of all those parts of *Land and Water* not written by himself! Writing to Maurice Baring on March 17, 1916, he observed:

'The non-Belloc part of *Land and Water* gets stupider and stupider every week. Even Mark Philipps, who is a first-rate man, is only allowed to write in it on condition that he talks of Prussia as a great big strong man, while everybody else is kind, good, and weak. Notably, I take it, the Senegalese. My feelings about *Land and Water* are mixed.

If it went to pieces it would not be able to pay me my contract money. On the other hand, if it became a large and permanent fortune I should regret having taken cash instead of shares.'[34]

If Vivian had known about this dismissal of the efforts of his colleagues and himself, he would doubtless have found the 'great man' insufferable.

At the end of 1916 Murray Allison approached Vivian with a new idea. He was going to launch a new magazine devoted to aviation. The aeroplane had suddenly proved itself during the war, from bumbling artillery 'spotter planes' they had become the very future of warfare and international travel. A subsidiary *Land and Water* company had been set up called Air Publishing Company Limited, at 5 Chancery Lane, WC2. With the first issue dated January 4, 1917, it would run as a weekly magazine on all matters of aviation. E. Charles Vivian was offered the job as editor. Within eight years of leaving the army as a lowly private, Vivian had worked on some of the most prestigious literary journals of the day, had published twelve books, many short stories and articles, and was now editor of what was to be the first and most influential general journal on aviation. Vivian was to be editor of it through its life until its penultimate issue on July 9, 1919.

In his first editorial, he stated:

'Ten years ago men did not fly—so rapidly has the change come upon us that no organ has yet appeared in this country proposing to deal with the general as well as the technical interests of flying, to explain and speak of it to the general reader, and to deal with the current problems for the expert.'[35]

Vivian signed many articles in the weekly publication but there are many other items which bear his touch. 'Letters of a Martian' viewing current politics'; 'Above the Clouds' by 'Icarus,' and the editorials signed 'Ariel'; all these show his style. Hilaire Belloc himself contributed as did Claude Farmer, Edgar Middleton and H. de Vere Stackpoole. H. de Vere Stacpoole became a bestselling Hutchinson author whose novel *The Blue Lagoon* (1919) was to sell a million copies within a few years of publication and to be made into a classic movie in 1949 starring Jean Simmons and Donald Houston and directed by Frank Launder. It was remade in Hollywood in 1980 with Brooke Shields and Christopher Atkins, directed by Randal Kleiser for Columbia. The remake was generally agreed to be terrible by critics and public alike.

Among the other contributors was an 'A. K. Walton' whom we can now identify as Vivian himself for some of Walton's stories, in Vivian style, were later rewritten and republished under Vivian's own name. Walton was also the name of a Cannell cousin.[36] The name 'Sydney Barr' also has the Vivian touch being a combination of favourite character names which he was to use in his fiction. Perhaps this was a foretaste of his later pseudonym '*Sydney Barr*ie Lynd'?

At the end of his first year as editor of *Flying*, Marion Vivian gave birth to a daughter at their Orchard Cottage. The child was born on October 25, 1917, and christened Katharine Marion Vivian. She was to become known as Kitty to the family. Vivian was now signing his official name as Charles Henry Vivian without the addition of 'otherwise Cannell' as he had on his marriage certificate, and describing himself as a journalist. But for his professional persona, he had established himself irrevocably as E. Charles Vivian.

It was in the columns of *Flying* that Vivian published, both as Vivian and Walton, some excellent weird stories, showing what apparently was his first steps into the genre. He also began a series of articles on the history of flying which became the basis of a book, a major 526 page *A History of Aeronautics*, published by William Collins in 1921. He had asked Lt. Col. W. Lochwood Marsh to contribute a section of aircraft design. This was the first single volume history of flying from legends of flight through the early experiments, through the vast developments during the war to 1920, the threshold of the age of flying. Among aviation experts, such as Sir Peter Masefield, (1914–2006) former director of Brooklands Museum, the volume was affectionately remembered as a first major step in aviation literature.[37] The book received an American edition from Harcourt but the *Saturday Review* felt: 'The author traces the work of the pioneers with competence but the book is attractive rather than academic, and will never attain the position of a standard authority.'[38]

Vivian's dedication to *A History of Aeronautics* throws up another mystery. It is dedicated 'to my witness, October 21, 1919. V.'. Why did Vivian need a witness on that date? It was his birthday and he was thirty-seven years old. Initially it was thought that this was a day when he might have legalised his change of name under a Deed Pole but this has been proved not so. At no time did Charles Henry Cannell ever change his name in law to Evelyn Charles Vivian. So the events of that birthday on the third Tuesday in October, 1919, remain a mystery.

Flying, which started off as a penny weekly, had become a six penny weekly by May 21, 1918, when The Field Press Ltd., of Windsor House, Bream Buildings, EC4, bought it from Allison's company. *Land and Water* was also incorporated with *The Field* in 1920. After the war had ended, Field Press decided to re-launch the publication as a glossy monthly. The July 9, 1919, issue was the last weekly issue and with it Vivian left the editorship. The new-look *Flying* had appeared with the August issue and immediately folded. The loyal readership did not approve of the change from its weekly format to the more expensive, glossy monthly. Vivian was now out of a job although he continued contributing items of journalism here and there and had some royalties from his published books. It was not until 1922 that he was invited to join the publishing company of Hutchinson & Co to originate and launch two popular fiction magazines. They were to be magazines to which his name was to become inseparably linked.

Notes

1. *Play Up and Play the Game*, Patrick Howarth, Eyre Methuen, London, 1973. See also *Tales Out of School*. Geoffrey Trease, Heinemann, London, 1949. Vivian, as a children's writer, is referred to in *The Men Behind Boy's Fiction*,

1. W. O. G. Lofts and D.J. Adley, Howard Baker, London, 1970.
2. Typical of Vivian's *Boys Own Paper* contributions are: 'The Little God with Moving Eyes: a Christmas Adventure in Rhodesia,' Vol. 36, p. 152, and 'Billy's Gun: A South African Adventure,' Vol 36, p 540 (1913/14) and 'Aztec Gold,' an adventure serial in Vol 42 (1919/20).
3. *Times Literary Supplement*, November 29, 1927.
4. *Times Literary Supplement*, November 24, 1927.
5. *Times Literary Supplement*, November 23, 1933.
6. 'On the Trail of the Mysterious Jack Mann' edited by W.O.G. Lofts, *Armchair Detective*, 1972, p. 20.
7. Mrs Katharine Ashton to author, November 4, 1990.
8. Mrs Katharine Ashton to author, January 13, 1993.
9. *Outlook* (USA) May 19, 1915.
10. *Wisconsin Library Bulletin*, February, 1915.
11. *The New York Times Review of Books*. October 11, 1914.
12. *Times Literary Supplement*, November 28, 1914. Even *The Asiatic Review* (January 1, 1915) devoted some space to reviewing it.
13. *Colour*, No 5, December, 1914.
14. *Review of Reviews* (UK), November, 1914.
15. *Land and Water*, October 24, 1914.
16. *Nation*, November 26, 1914.
17. *Review of Reviews* (USA) December, 1914.
18. *The New York Times Review of Books*, November 8, 1914.
19. For the activities of Wellington House, see *Great War of Words*, Peter Buitenhuis, c. 1985.
20. *Land and Water*, November 28, 1914.
21. p.78 of *Living Memories*, John Attenborough, Hodder and Stoughton, London, 1975.
22. *New York Times*, June 27, 1915, see also *Nation*, August 12, 1915.
23. *Boston Transcript*, September 22, 1915.
24. *Colour*, February, 1915, and, *The Asiatic Review*, noticed it in their April, 1, 1915, issue.
25. *Times Literary Supplement*, March 4, 1915.
26. *Land and Water*, January 30, 1915.
27. *Independent* (USA) October 4, 1915.

28. *New York Times Review of Books*, September 26, 1915.
29. *Athenaeum*, February 12, 1916.
30. *Nation*, September 9, 1915.
31. *Hilaire Belloc*, A.N. Wilson, Hamish Hamilton, London, 1984 p. 223.
32. *The Life of Hilaire Belloc*. Robert Speaight, Hollis & Carter, London, 1957, p. 347.
33. *A General Sketch of the European War: The First Phrase* Hilaire Belloc, Nelson, London, 1915, pp. 370/377.
34. *The Life of Hilaire Belloc*. Speaight, p. 355.
35. *Flying*, June 4, 1917.
36. A.M. Walton MBE to author, September 8, 1991.
37. Sir Peter Masefield, director of The Brooklands Museum, formerly Chief Executive of British European Airways and Chairman of the British Airports Authority, in conversation with the author at Brooklands, October 20, 1993.

CHAPTER FIVE

ADVENTURE AND MYSTERY

Joining Hutchinson & Co in Paternoster Row, EC4, during the spring or summer of 1922, Vivian was to begin a period of three years of frenetic activity with a vast outpouring of serials and short stories together with eleven books published. In addition, he was a full-time Hutchinson editor. His main brief was to devise, launch and edit *Hutchinson's Adventure-Story Magazine* and *Hutchinson's Mystery-Story Magazine*, soon to become two popular fiction 'pulps' that have become 'fabled' among aficionados. The period was to be the pinnacle of Vivian's career as a journalist and the start of his new career as a genre fiction writer of repute. By this time Vivian, his wife Marion and daughter Kitty were living in Ashtead in Surrey and he was commuting into London.[1] Vivian had also become a keen motorist, a member of the Royal Automobile Club. 'He liked looking after cars—finding the sources of rattles, improving a car's performance and so forth,' recalled his daughter.[2] He used to drive a Wolseley saloon at this time but bought a Vauxhall in the 1930s. He would often drive his family for vacations in the West Country. His daughter recalled staying once at Woolacombe in Devon which was just a few miles along the coast from Wood Bay where Vivian has his character 'Beth', in *Ash*, die in isolation. It is clear that Vivian knew this area fairly well.

The Hutchinson Publishing Company had been founded in 1887 by George Thompson Hutchinson (1857–1931), knighted in 1912 for his services to publishing. The company soon expanded, publishing everything from popular fiction to educational works and specialising in large format part-works. The company also moved quickly into the magazine business and their earliest popular success was launched in November, 1896, in the shape of *The Lady's Realm*. *The Lady's Realm* was sold to Stanley Paul in November, 1909. He licensed it to Amalgamated Press but it ceased publication in May, 1916.

In the year that Sir George formed his publishing company, his wife gave birth to his only son, Walter Victor Hutchinson. Sir Robert Lusty, who worked for him between 1928 and 1935, devoted a chapter to Walter in his autobiography *Bound to Be Read*[3] where he describes him as 'one of the strangest and... one of the saddest enigmas to bestride the publishing scene of his day'. The critic and literary historiographer Jack Adrian is a little kinder while referring to him as 'the eccentric Walter Hutchinson'. He says 'Walter Hutchinson was a man of genuinely inspired ideas, which, however, often went some way beyond what his innate parsimony would allow.'[4] Mike Ashley confirms that 'Walter Hutchinson has not gone down in history as one of the world's best-liked men'.[5]

Ashley, in fact, is a harsh critic:

'Walter Hutchinson was an eccentric despot who had no clear inkling of what he was trying to achieve, and so sought to do everything. He established his company as one of the largest in the world probably the largest in terms of the volume of books published. The books were almost always cheaply produced, of little lasting quality, but were ideal for a readership of transient interests, and they sold in their millions. Yet Hutchinson was not as liberal with the proceeds. Lusty reports a remark of Hutchinson's which has become legendary. When asked by a senior employee for a raise of five or ten shillings a week (then about one or two dollars), Walter snorted the response: "Don't you know it costs me three pounds a week to feed one of my horses?"'[6]

Walter was educated at public school and sent to university for a legal training. He took his master's degree, won several academic honours and was called to the bar, all before his twenty-fourth birthday. At that age, he forsook law and joined the family firm in 1911. His father soon gave him the main controlling interest in the company and he became managing director. His only interest outside the company was as a racehorse owner and bloodstock breeder. He was also a 'gentleman farmer'.

In 1919, when war restrictions on paper had eased, Walter Hutchinson foresaw the subsequent boom in periodical publishing. In July, 1919, he launched *Hutchinson's Story Magazine*, selling at ninepence for a 128 page standard 'pulp'. In May, 1921, the magazine was re-titled simply *Hutchinson's* Magazine. This 'flagship' of Hutchinson's magazine empire, was soon joined by the *Sovereign Magazine*, launched in 1919. Then Hutchinson began publishing British editions of American 'pulps' such as *True-Story* and *True-Love Stories*. He added to these *The Smart Set* and *Action Stories*. By 1925, the range of magazines had grown from the weekly *Light (A Journal of Spiritual Progress and Psychical Research)* to the monthly *The Writer*, devoted to the interests of coming journalists and authors; on the more popular front he had launched *Woman and Physical Culture*.

Walter Hutchinson had originally devoted *Hutchinson Magazine* to serialisations of the books he was to publish and with occasional short stories. The first issue included Haggard's *She Meets Allan*, as well as stories by H. de Vere Stacpoole, whose verses Vivian had published in *Flying*. After a while, the serials were cut down as Hutchinson realised the interest in shorter fiction. The *Sovereign*, when he launched it, specialised in adventure stories and short fiction from such luminaries as Achmed Abdullah (author of *The Thief of Baghdad*), Rafael Sabatini, Sax Rohmer, Edison Marshall, and Edgar Rice Burroughs. Burroughs appeared in the March, 1920, issue with '*An Eye for an Eye*,' the first of six stories which were to form the novel *Tarzan the Untamed*. Sabatini's classic *Scaramouche* began serialisation in *Sovereign* in November, 1920.

As he sought to build up this magazine empire, Walter Hutchinson was busy acquiring companies. It seemed that he had a passion for buying out publishing companies who were in financial difficulties due to wartime problems. Among the 160 companies he acquired were Hurst & Blackett, Jarrolds, Stanley Paul, Skeffington, Rider & Co., and Selwyn Blount.

According to Jack Adrian:

'Most of Walter Hutchinson's magazines were heavily dependent on fiction; but in 1923 he changed course, transforming *Hutchinson's* into an enlarged 'fine art' production printed on heavy stock. The best popular authors and journalists wrote for him, the best commercial artists provided illustrations. In this Hutchinson again showed his shrewdness by anticipating—and influencing—such later best-selling general interest magazines as *Nash's Pall Mall*, *Woman's Journal*, and *Britannia and Eve*. Hutchinson's incorrigible penny-pinching sabotaged the enterprise and by the end of the decade all that remained was *Hutchinson's* itself, no longer printed on art stock, drastically reduced in dimensions, and visibly moribund. Few first-rank writers now contributed to it, and what illustrations there were appeared to be the work of an office junior.'[7]

But this was in the future. Against the exciting, feverish activities of Walter Hutchinson, during the post war years, E. Charles Vivian was persuaded to join the company for the specific purpose of planning, launching and editing two more magazines for Walter's growing fiction magazine empire.

By this time Vivian had become, in addition to regular appearances in *Colour*, an occasional contributor to Odham's *Pan* and its companion *Twenty-Story Magazine*. Various stories and articles from his typewriter were also appearing in a variety of publications from *Chamber's Journal*, *The Sketch* to the *Windsor Magazine*.

The first issue of *Adventure-Story Magazine* was launched in September, 1922. Mike Ashley says it was 'the first specialised fiction "pulp" in Britain outside the women's magazines'.[8] Its basic theme was adventure stories. It may well be that Vivian was influenced by the famous American 'pulp' *Adventure*, launched in November, 1910, and which lasted well into the 1950s. *Adventure*'s first editor was the talented Arthur Sullivant Hoffman whose discerning eye for good stories and quality writing caused such demand that the former monthly was issued three times monthly during the 1920s. Certainly some of the stories in *Adventure-Story* first appeared in the US *Adventure*, According to Ashley: 'It's quite possible that it was the success and format of *Adventure* that gave Hutchinson the idea for his own *Adventure-Story.*' [9]

The first issue saw Vivian using H. Bedford-Jones, Oscar Cook, C. M. Eddy, Edison Marshall and Sapper. With Walter Hutchinson's penny-pinching attitude, Vivian was doubtless asked to use as much of his own material in the magazine as he could. The result was somewhat startling. Vivian began to crank the handle on a wealth of well-written stories and serials not only under the name of Vivian but as Galbraith Nicholson, Sydney Barrie Lynd and A.K. Walton. The exact number of pen names that he used will probably never be known but there are many pseudonymous names in the pages of both magazines that may be attributed to him. 'E. Hope Samson' seems to leap at one. Both 'Hope' and 'Samson' are names occurring in Vivian stories and, bearing this in mind, 'E. Hope Samson' does not become too far removed from E. Charles Vivian. Other names have been easy to identify. Galbraith Nicholson, for example. The New York based *Golden Fleece*, a magazine devoted to historical adventure, published 'Count Caspar' as a novella, in their May, 1939, issue, revealing the author as E. Charles Vivian. Vivian had first published this under the name 'Galbraith Nicholson' as a serial in *Adventure-Story* from December, 1923, through to May, 1924. Sydney Barrie Lynd (Lynd was also used as a character in a Vivian novel), changed to Barrie Lynd, wrote many stories in *Adventure-Story* and *Mystery-Story*. Vivian changed the name again to Barry Lynd when he wrote half-a-dozen western novels between 1938 and 1942. 'A.K. Walton' was the name he had used in *Flying* and some Walton stories he republished under the name Vivian.

For the first issue of *Adventure-Story* Vivian began a serialisation of a 'lost race' fantasy under his own name entitled *City of Wonder*.

City of Wonder immediately won Vivian a following and showed that he was able to produce an adventure story which could be compared with the best of H. Rider Haggard's 'lost race' tales. Narrated by Jack Faulkner, the adventure told how Faulkner, Philip Watkins and Cecil Bent comes to Kir-Asa, 'most remotely secure of all the world's secret places since man began to make history, away in the wilds that still exist in certain lands of the Pacific'. They are tracing the steps of an earlier expedition led by Watkins' ancestor in 1768. The story starts when the three are on the verge of discovering the entrance to Kir-Asa, through 'the place where the ghosts chase women', through an encounter with a woman who commands the obedience of savage apes, to the discovery of the lost civilisation.

Because they have killed The Nantia and her savage apes, who guard the entrance to their civilisation, the people of Kir-Asa take the explorers before Saya Comin, their congenitally mad king. Faulkner and Eve, daughter of a nobleman, Ner-Ag, fall in love. But Saya Comin, the king, wants Eve for himself. There is a coup d'etat, Saya Comin is killed, and Ner-Ag is acclaimed leader while Macer, the equally mad son of Saya Comin, seeks battle. Defeated he flees, but kills Eve in the process. Faulkner swears vengeance and pursues Macer beyond the secret valley. Faulkner returns to civilisation a broken man and, dying, writes down his adventure.

With *City of Wonder* it seemed that Vivian had broken off the constraints of his previous 'serious' work and had given full range to his incredibly fertile imagination, earning himself a justified reputation as an exciting new fantasy writer. Hutchinson published *City of Wonder* in book form as soon as the serial ended in January, 1923, while the firm of Moffatt issued an American edition. Hutchinson reprinted the book in a cheaper edition in February, 1924, in a series of what was now named '*Adventure-Story Library*'. It was still being reprinted in the US by Centaur Press of New York, in a popular paperback edition, in 1973, fifty years after its first publication.

Vivian was now working on the format of the second magazine he was to launch, *Mystery-Story Magazine*. This was to be even more specialised, concentrating on weird, ghost, mystery, and crime stories only. The first issue was to be launched in February, 1923, with the same 96 page format as *Adventure-Story*, priced at seven pence. Both magazines were published on the 16th of the month prior to cover date.

The first issue of *Mystery-Story* did not have quite the same impressive group of writers in the first issue as *Adventure-Story*. Some names became better known later, such as Arthur Hutchinson, no kin to Walter, who was editor of Ward Lock's *Windsor Magazine*, also Frederick C. Davis, Isabel Ostrander and Robert Murray Graydon. Alas, many early issues of *Mystery-Story* have disappeared from the archives. They are not even held by copyright libraries.

Vivian now seemed a veritable powerhouse of production. He was producing serials and short stories for both his magazines.

A few months after *City of Wonder* had finished its serialisation, Vivian began to serialise *Fields of Sleep* in *Adventure-Story*, between May and October, 1923. Once again he had produced a powerful 'lost race' tale. Indeed, it was an important book for Vivian. The story has Victor Marshall hired by Madame Delarey to find her son Clement who has disappeared into a remote and unexplored part of Asia. Clement's sister, strong willed, insists on accompanying Marshall and thus provides the romance. Marshall's path leads him to a lost valley whose inhabitants are descended from ancient Chaldean colonists. They are dependent upon a narcotic flower whose fragrance produces a strange ecstasy while destroying the power of speech. A young Michael Joseph, then a critic on *Smart Set*, hailed it as 'one of the greatest works of modern imaginative fiction.'[10] Joseph was later to establish his own famous publishing house.

Fields of Sleep was published by Hutchinson in July, 1923, and reprinted in 1925. However, it did not reach an American audience until August, 1949, when *Famous Fantastic Mysteries Magazine* published it as 'The Valley of Silent Men.' Not until 1980 did Donald M. Grant Publisher Inc. produce a US edition under its original title.

Vivian's frenzied energy was now not confined to the two magazines which he was editing. He was now producing short stories for other Hutchinson magazines, *Sovereign*, *Smart Set*, *Woman*, and even for the 'flagship' publication *Hutchinson's Magazine*. It was a period of incredible activity. Cynically, this may well be due to the terms of his contract with Walter Hutchinson who probably insisted that his editors use as much of their own material as possible and spread it throughout all his publications rather than pay high prices to more established writers. Vivian was now financially secure from his writing income.

In 1923 Vivian had five novels published in book form, together with two serials as Galbraith Nicholson, one as Vivian and something in the region of a score of short stories.

In 1923 he produced two 'serious' works which he persuaded Hutchinson to publish in book form. Because of his success with 'lost race' fantasy as E. Charles Vivian, it was doubtless Walter Hutchinson who suggested that he should find another name. Vivian returned to his original name and the first 'Charles Cannell' novels were published. *The Guarded Woman* appeared in April and *Broken Couplings* in August.

The Guarded Woman begins with two fraudulent managers of a financial company in the City being tracked down by the hero, a secretive and mysterious young foreigner who becomes secretary to the company. Then Vivian switches tack and plunges into a Ruritanian romance with the hero, representative of a small state, engaging the villains, employed by a rival state. The *Times Literary Supplement*[11] felt 'this tale embodies an unfortunate mixture of manners'. Vivian was clearly intent on character development and human relationships.

With *Broken Couplings* 'Charles Cannell' had a little more success. Gerald Newton has married Ellen Woollaston believing her first husband to be dead. But the husband, Cecil Woollaston, had only abandoned her when she had become an alcoholic. He now reappears from America. There are complications as the story involves gold prospecting in Copper Creek in Canada, where Newton and his friend, Tolway, head. Cecil Woollaston winds up being mangled by a wheel and Ellen, cured from her alcoholism is able to face the future with Gerald Newton. While attempting to present 'serious novels', Vivian seems to find it difficult to avoid the introduction of adventure themes.

While the *Times Literary Supplement* assessed it as a melodramatic story[12] other publications were more welcoming. *The Guardian* felt it was 'a good piece of work, interesting alike in love and adventure'; the *Graphic* thought 'the action is rapid and full of interest', while the *Newcastle Times* enigmatically observed that it was 'a much changing drama'.[13] Unlike *The Guarded Woman*, Hutchinson's produced a reprint of *Broken Couplings* in January, 1927.

Broken Couplings was dedicated 'with sincere regard' to the author Sheila Kaye-Smith (1887–1956). She has been claimed for Sussex as Thomas Hardy was for Wessex. Her Sussex set novels had, by this time, earned her a deserved reputation. Once more it is a mystery how her path crossed with Vivian for she certainly did not contribute to any publication he edited. In 1924 she was to marry Theodore Penrose Fry, an Anglican rector at St Leonard's. In 1929 they both converted to Catholicism and Fry inherited a baronetcy, becoming Sir Penrose Fry. Vivian's daughter says: 'I do not think my parents knew her personally.'[14]

So great was Vivian's output during this year, that one stands amazed that he was additionally editing the two monthly magazines as well as writing. According to Ashley:

'E. Charles Vivian was a very able editor for *Mystery-Story*. He brought a good balance of mystery and weird stories to the magazine, and it is not without some truth that the magazine has been considered the closest "pulp" to *Weird Tales* produced in Britain. Vivian, in all likelihood, saw issues of *Weird Tales*, and it is a little surprising that he never contributed to the magazine (unless further pseudonyms come to light). During his editorship, though, whilst he drew heavily upon *Adventure* for *Adventure-Story*, most of the stories he purchased for *Mystery-Story* were new, or came from Street & Smith's *Detective Story Magazine*.'[15]

Vivian had created an individualistic style for *Mystery-Story*. Hutchinson's sensationalist book jackets were translated to brash covers, with the September, 1923, issue offering a £10 prize for the best story to be written, in 2,000 words, around the cover illustration. The winner of this first contest was Claire D. Pollexfen

(1884–1974), a cousin of the poet W. B. Yeats, with 'Three Gentlemen from the North.'[16] She went on to become a regular contributor to *Mystery-Story* with eight stories and a novel. She became well respected, contributing to a wide variety of magazines in the late 1920s and 1930s. She also became a friend of Vivian's. Vivian was to dedicate two books to her as late as 1941. In *And Then There Was One* the dedication reads: 'To Claire—it all comes to the same thing in the end—Vivian. 2.11.40.' Even more mysterious is the dedication in *Her Ways Are Death*: 'To Claire because of Peter, and . . . G. 4.12.40.' Why the initial 'G'? And did Claire posses a cherry coloured cat named Peter as such a cat called Peter appears in the book belonging to the witch Ira with whom the hero falls in love?

Names that have become familiar to devotees of weird fiction began to appear under Vivian's careful editorship. Arlton Eadie, pen name of Leopold Eady (1886–1935), and G. G. Pendarves, whose real name was Gladys Gordon Trenery (1885–1938), were two of the more colourful personalities to be published by him.

Yet, while reading and choosing stories for his two monthly publications, Vivian continued his amazingly prodigious output. He excelled himself in 1924 by publishing two novels, three serials and nearly forty short stories while writing a regular literary column for *Smart Set*. His first book of the year, published in April, was another stunning 'lost race' tale, which, in fact, was a direct sequel to *Fields of Sleep*. This was *People of Darkness*, which had been serialised in *Adventure-Story* from February to May, 1924. The second book was another Charles Cannell title: *Barker's Drift*, an adventure tale which had a moderate success being reprinted in 1926 and then issued under Vivian's own name in 1936 by Ward Lock.

It was in March, 1924, that Vivian met a twenty-three old married woman named Lillian Simmons. She had been born in Fulham, London, in 1901, as Lillian East. She had married a local council clerk, Clarence George Simmons, also from Fulham, in Camberwell in 1920. He was three years younger. She was later to relate that she had been by herself in a restaurant when Vivian came in. There was a vacant seat beside her which he took. Being young and attractive doubtless Vivian opened a conversation. He told her he was an author and a friend of Rider Haggard. Young Lillian was obviously impressed. She was not a 'shrinking violet' and certainly had at least one other affair, booking rooms in an inn in Buckinghamshire as a place of assignation. However, she insisted that there was no intimacy in her relationship with Vivian until 1926.[17]

But at the beginning of 1925 Vivian told her that he was going to Paris to get material for a book based in the Parisian underworld. She claimed that he asked her for a loan and that she had given him £66. Certainly, her background was not one which would indicate that she, or indeed, her husband, could have access to this sum, judging by their backgrounds and Clarence Simmons job. Eight years after this incident, Clarence Simmons was still only earning £4 a week, living in a house rented at 8 shillings a week in Fort Road, Bermondsey, SE1. And why would Vivian, a successful author and editor at this time, need to ask such a girl for money? Certainly, he had made a substantial income in 1924. Yet years later the story would be believed by a judge and jury.

Certainly, by the end of 1924 Vivian had planned to take his family to France and settle there for a while, giving up his editorships and journalism and relying on his income from his books. If one judges by the abrupt halt of the appearance of his stories in *Adventure-Story* in January, 1925, and the easing off of his considerable output in other Hutchinson magazines in the early part of that year, we have a good argument that he left Hutchinson in late 1924. Vivian's daughter remembers the year of the departure to France as 1924.

This is also confirmed by another source. Christine Campbell Thomson was now an editor at Roger Ingpen's failing imprint, Selwyn & Blount. She had met the writer Oscar Cook (1888–1952), a former District Officer in British North Borneo from 1911 to 1919, while she had been employed as a reader at Curtis Brown. Cook had written for Vivian in both *Adventure-Story* and *Mystery-Story*. Miss Thomson and Oscar Cook married on September 30, 1924, and she recalled that immediately after the marriage Cook joined Walter Hutchinson to replace Vivian as editor.[18]

'Vivian may well have recommended Cook', Ashley concedes. Cook left the editorship in 1926 and bought out Roger Ingpen at Selwyn & Blount to become managing director of the firm. Coincidentally, Walter Hutchinson then bought out his erstwhile editor and acquired Selwyn & Blount in 1933. With Cook at the helm of Selwyn & Blount, Christine Thomson became famous for a series of weird anthologies, the *Not at Night Series* produced for the firm. Curiously, in the fifteen or so volumes, not one Vivian weird tale appears. It was these volumes which inspired Hutchinson to produce his mammoth 'Century of...' anthologies. Cook and Christine Thomson were divorced in 1938 and Cook died in 1952. It was an acrimonious parting with much bitterness, for Christine, in her autobiography, can write about her career with hardly a reference to Cook.

Before he set out for France, Vivian had made sure that he had several projects in the publishing pipeline. While he left ten short stories, written for *Smart Set*, to be published throughout 1925, he had four more books ready for publication. But only two of these books were to be published by Hutchinson. This sudden lack of support, both from the Hutchinson magazines and on the book publishing side, may indicate that when Vivian left, Walter Hutchinson's good wishes did not go with him, or that simply he did not want to pay for Vivian's prolific material. There is another suggestion. Vivian had decided that being abroad, and removed from the centre of publishing, it would be a wise idea to have a literary agent. He chose John Farquharson, who had founded his agency in 1919. It may well be that it was Farquharson who ended the relationship with Hutchinson in his attempts to get a better deal for his author.

Vivian's last two books for Hutchinson were as different from each other as one could get. Firstly, in January, 1925, as Charles Cannell, he published *Ash*. This was, as has already been discussed, Vivian's major attempt to come to terms with the problems of his unhappy childhood by presenting a fictionalised autobiographical work. It did go to a cheap reprint in March, 1926, but was not especially noticed by the critics. Nevertheless, as an explanation of boy and man, *Ash* was one of Vivian's most important works.

In March, it was back to genre fiction with Vivian producing *Star Dust*. The story assumed the discovery of a new source of power, and therefore verges on science fiction rather than fantasy. Leonard Ferrers has made a machine with which he can control weather and, among other demonstrations, he raises a storm which devastates Surrey, the county where Vivian was then living. Even in this story, Ferrers is the product of an unhappy relationship with his father who married the again after the death of his mother. Ferrers aims to destabilise governments by putting 'synthetic' gold on the market. Ferrers and his wife are eventually killed. The *Times Literary Supplement* was moved to comment: 'Extravagant as it is, the tale is amusing and at times interesting.'[19]

Farquharson had sold the next two books to Vivian's erstwhile non-fiction publisher, Hodder & Stoughton. Towards the end of the year, Hodder & Stoughton published *The Guardian of the Cup*. While this was written as Charles Cannell it was more in the new Vivian grand oriental adventure style. The cup of Wu Ti, a priceless antique, is stolen, having been in the custody of Dr Evelyn Hill, a female doctor, who controls a hospital in an old temple in North China. With a terrible smallpox epidemic raging, and the help of a Chinese assistant doctor Sun Wei, she attempts to make the mission hospital cope. John Collier, a mining engineer and adventurer, is sent by Ut Lee to find the cup which is in the temple. There is a rival in Hugh Seldon for Evelyn's love and nasty villains in the persons of Messrs Woolner and Lebert who are also after the cup. It is certainly more of the staple fare of Vivian rather than the 'serious' Mr Cannell. Indeed, in 1935, Ward Lock reprinted the book under the E. Charles Vivian by-line.

Hodder & Stoughton then issued a Vivian title in December, which was another 'lost race' fantasy: *The Lady of the Terraces*. This was certainly on a par to the major 'lost race' novels which he had published by Hutchinson. Colvin Barr is persuaded to go on a gold hunting expedition in the Andes. His companion is Felippe

Guttierez, the Torrero of Guayaquil. They head into the Araueros Range and are captured by natives. A strange birthmark on Barr is identified by the natives as the mark of royal Caras, and it is announced that Barr is 'he of the foretelling because of the birthmark on his breast'. There is a villain in Huello but Barr wins the heart and hand of the wise and beautiful Queen Caris, the last survivor of the royal line. He is accepted by this 'lost race' as their king. But Huello bedevils him and in an epic cliff-top struggle both Barr and Huello go over to their doom together, leaving the beautiful Caris and faithful Felippe inconsolable. The *Times Literary Supplement* was impressed. 'Though the author is a little slow getting into his stride, he makes ample amends once he does so, and the result is a stirring and romantic story.'[20]

With his departure, Vivian had bequeathed Hutchinson two magazines that were already popular sellers. But times were becoming difficult. Within a year the depression and General Strike were affecting Hutchinson's magazines. The kind of readers that the Hutchinson's 'pulps' were aimed at had no money to spare on the luxury of magazines. In spite of the economic signs, Walter Hutchinson continued to over-reach himself. In July, 1925, he launched *Standard Stories*. This publication lasted until its May, 1926, issue and has become a rarity for the entire run held by the British Library has been destroyed. Similarly, *Best Story Magazine* were launched and then disappeared. *The Regent Magazine* was combined with *The Sovereign* as *The Jolly Magazine*, perhaps in an attempt to bring a bright face to the depression. With the October, 1927, issue, *Adventure-Story* and *Mystery-Story* were merged into one magazine which sadly saw its final issue with June, 1929. Indeed, 1929, the year Vivian returned from France, saw the end of the short but influential range of Hutchinson's 'pulp' magazines. By December of that year, all the titles had folded. It was the end of a magazine publishing phenomenon in which Vivian had made an effective contribution.

This was, of course, in the future for by the Spring of 1925 E. Charles Vivian was a resident in the suburb of Boulogne-sur-Seine in Paris, not far from the Bois de Boulogne.

Notes

1. Katharine Vivian Ashton to author, October 12, 1991.
2. Katharine Vivian Ashton to author, June 10, 1994.
3. *Bound to Be Read*, Robert Lusty, Jonathan Cape, London, 1975.
4. *Desirable Residences and other stories*, E.F. Benson, Introduction by Jack Adrian, Oxford University Press, 1991. (see pp. x and xi).
5. 'The Trail of Adventure and Mystery: Uncovering the Hutchinson Pulp Magazines' by Mike Ashley (*Pulp Vault*, No 10, 1992).
6. *Ibid*.
7. see *Desirable Residences* (above).
8. 'The Trail of Adventure . . . etc' Ashley (above).
9. *Ibid*.
10. *Smart Set*, October, 1923.
11. *Times Literary Supplement*, April 26, 1923.
12. *Times Literary Supplement*, September 12, 1923.
13. *The Guardian*, September 13, 1923; *The Graphic*, September 16, 1923 and *Newcastle Times*, September 12, 1923.
14. Katharine Vivian Ashton to author, June 8, 1994.
15. 'Unlocking the Night,' Mike Ashley, pp. 178-185 in *Gaslight and Ghosts* edited by Stephen Jones & Jo Fletcher, 1988 World Fantasy Convention and Robinson Publishing, London, 1988.
16. December, 1923.
17. *The Times*, January 14, 1933.
18. 'Unlocking the Night' (see above): see also *I am a Literary Agent: Memories Personal and Professional*, by Christine Campbell Thomson, Sampson Low & Marston, London, 1951.
19. *Times Literary Supplement*, April 18, 1925.
20. *Times Literary Supplement*, December 17, 1925.

CHAPTER SIX

FRANCE

Vivian's four year period in France is, like many areas of his life, also shrouded with some degree of mystery. Why did he suddenly go to France? Was it anything to do with Lillian Simmons? There are other matters that do not fit into Vivian's daughter's account that the family remained in France for several years. If we are to believe Mrs Simmons, and a judge and jury did in 1933, she began having an affair with Vivian from 1926. She had, she claimed, given him £66 before he left for Paris in 1924. She then said that in 1926 he told her that he had written a play *The Guarded Woman*. His novel with this title had appeared in April, 1923, but under Charles Cannell. He had said he needed to back it with £100. She lent him £50 and then pawned her jewellery and raised a further £40. This without demur from a housewife whose husband was bringing in, at that time, less than £4 a week. Mrs Simmons says she continued her affair with Vivian until 1928, after which 'they lost sight of each other' and she did not get her money back.[1]

One interesting problem that never was answered in court was how did Vivian keep up this affair while living in France with his family, while Mrs Simmons remained in Bermondsey with her husband? Vivian's daughter says: 'We went to Paris—my parents and I—about 1924; after a year or two, went to stay in St Jean-de-Luz where we met the writer J. D. Beresford and his family. A few years later we returned to England and lived in Horsham.'[2]

The interesting fact is that, according to an interview given to Haycraft and Kunitz for *Twentieth Century Authors* (1942), J. D. Beresford also says that he went to France in 1925, returned to England in 1929 and then went to live in Horsham. This is contradicted by his son Marcus who says his father took the family to France in 1923 and returned to England in September 1928. But if J. D. Beresford's statement is right then the dates coincided with the dates that Vivian took his family to France. Kitty Vivian says 'The writer J. D. Beresford was a close friend of his' (Vivian's)[3] But when did that friendship begin? Was it prior to their being neighbours in St-Jean-de-Luz? Indeed, if the dates given by J. D. Beresford are right one might wonder whether the two men actually planned the whole of their sojourn in France together? Beresford was certainly in Paris in 1926 for his youngest child, Elizabeth Beresford (later to become creator of the 'Wombles', the bestselling children's books) was born there in that year. And Vivian and his family were also in Paris that year. Elizabeth explained that her father hated bureaucracy and did not register her birth but that her mother, in later years, obtained a letter from the mayor of Neuilly-sur-Seine confirming her birth in that department. Of course, Neuilly-sur-Seine was a short distance from where the Vivians were living.[4]

One place where the paths of Beresford and Vivian might have crossed before France was at the offices of William Collins. Beresford was an editorial consultant for the firm between 1918 and 1923, and in 1921 Vivian had published his *A History of Aeronautics* with them. While aviation was hardly a common concern, both men were writers of weird fantasy tales, which was a point of mutual interest.

But if the dates and memories of Marcus are accurate, there is an end to such speculation. He speaks of a period on the Riviera before a move to St Jean-de-Luz and then a move to Paris, which would mean that the paths of Beresford and Vivian would have crossed in St Jean-de-Luz for only a matter of months early in 1926.

John Davys Beresford had been born at Castor, Northants, on March 7 1873. He was the son of a rector. Infantile paralysis, contracted when he was three years old, caused him to remain lame throughout his life. He had married Beatrice Roskans and, at the time he went to France, he had three sons, Tristram, Marcus (Mark Brandel, the writer) and Aden. His first novel *Jacob Stahl* had been published in 1911, but he is now best remembered for his weird fantasy such as his shorter fiction 'The Hampendshire Wonder' (1911) and 'The Camberwell Miracle' (1933). His short fiction tended to underline the nastiness found in people. His two most often reprinted stories are 'The Misanthrope' and 'Cut Throat Farm' both appearing in his collection *Nineteen Impressions* (1918).

There is another intriguing link between Vivian and his 'close friend' J. D. Beresford. They both shared the same literary agent in the person of John Farquharson.

Elizabeth Beresford believes there is a good reason why it has been difficult to trace a record of the Beresford/Vivian friendship. Not only did Vivian's apartment get bombed in the war but when Elizabeth was about ten years old, J. D. Beresford left home with a neighbour, the novelist Esme Wynne-Tyson. Esme (1898–1972) was born Dorothy Estelle Esme Ripper and started a career as an actress under the name Esme Wynne. By a curious coincidence, in view of the relevance of the name to Vivian, she was the original Rosamund in 'Where the Rainbow Ends' (1911). She wrote several plays and collaborated with Noel Coward. Her first novel *Security* appeared in 1926. At the time she became friendly with J. D. Beresford she was married to Wing-Commander Lynden C. Wynne-Tyson, and had a son, Jon. Beatrice Beresford was angered and burnt all her husband's papers, diaries and even his own books. Esme was to co-author three books with Beresford. Only once did Elizabeth Beresford, unbeknown to her family, 'sneak off', as she put it, to visit her father, which was at the age of seventeen, a few years before he died.[5] Esme Wynne-Tyson's son, Jon, remembered the name E. Charles Vivian, and knew of his works, but could not give details of his friendship with J. D. Beresford.[6]

When Vivian went to Paris, he not only took his wife Marion and daughter Kitty, who was aged seven, but he took his youngest sister, Olive Cannell. According to Vivian's daughter: 'My aunt Olive came with us to Paris as governess for me.'[7] Olive Louise, depicted under the name 'Iris' in *Ash*, was a schoolteacher. In *Ash*, as in real life. Olive had inherited some of the Cannell Nonconformist religious values and when she died in 1960 she left a bequest to the Nonconformist London City Mission at 6 Eccleston Street, London, SW1.

Olive was a thirty-eight year old spinster when she accompanied her brother's family to Paris. According to Vivian's daughter: 'She was going to be married and I was to be a bridesmaid, but it did not come to anything and I think she took up nursing.'[8] The details were not recalled, as 'people's private affairs, such as Aunt Olive's broken engagement, would not be discussed in front of the children/ servants.'[9] In fact, Olive appears to have returned to England when the Vivians left Paris for the south of France in order to nurse her mother. Louisa Anne Cannell died on February 7, 1929, at her home at 5 Irvine Terrace, Cliffe, near Strood. Olive was present at the death and gave details to the local registrar. After that, Olive moved to Teddington, south of London, and resumed her teaching career. She was never married. She died from cerebral thrombosis on August 5 1960, aged 74, at a hospital in Thornton Heath. In those final years, she had been living at Flat 9, White Hall, 250 South Norwood Hill, SE25, and had remained in touch with her nephew, her sister's son 'Alan' Charles Clarke who became her executor.

Vivian had rented an apartment in the department of Boulogne-sur-Seine, a suburb of Paris and not far from the Bois de Boulogne and adjacent to Neuilly-sur-Seine, where the Beresfords were living by the summer of 1926.

Sometime in 1926 Vivian took his family down to the French Basque country; to the town of St Jean-de-Luz not far from the Spanish border. 'At St Jean-de-Luz, we were at a pension called the Villa des Quartre Soisons, run by a Maori woman (a princess it was said), Phoebe Pitcairn.'[10] The name would place Phoebe as a Polynesian descendant of the famous *Bounty* mutineers rather than a Maori. It is an irrelevant piece of interesting information that Fletcher Christian of the *Bounty*, who led his mutineers to settle on Pitcairn, was a member of the famous Christian family of the Isle of

Man. Vivian, too, was the great-grandson of Manx seamen. Perhaps it was a subject of conversation between Vivian and his landlady? Or perhaps Vivian had even rejected this aspect of his background? Certainly he seemed to have an awareness of Celtic mythology and folk traditions, as exemplified in *Grey Shapes* (1937), which might have been handed down from his Gaelic-speaking great— grandfather.

At St Jean-de-Luz, the Vivians and Beresfords were certainly neighbours and friends. Kitty Vivian says she often saw the Beresford children, Tristram, Aden, and Mark. She used to play with the elder boys, Tristram and Aden. In fact, she remained friendly with Tristram and in later years Tristram and his wife were neighbours of Kitty Vivian and her husband at Presteigne in Wales. Marcus Beresford, however, has no recollection at all of Vivian or his family.[11] His remembrance was that the Beresford family moved to St Jean-de-Luz in the winter of 1925 and moved to Paris by August, 1926, when Elizabeth was born.

In 1929 the Vivians returned to England. 'Why we went back to England, I don't know,' Kitty admits.[12] Could the return have been caused by the death of Vivian's mother in February of that year? Kitty Vivian does not think so. She believed that her father had had no contact with his parents since he ran away from home as a teenager. Equally as important is the question why did Vivian chose to set up home in Horsham, a town that was certainly not in Vivian's previous orbit. Is it simply coincidence that J. D. Beresford and his family had returned to England that same year and also set up home in Horsham? That is, if we accept the statement of J. D. Beresford. According to Marcus Beresford, the family returned in September, 1928, going first to Poole, in Dorset, then to Bournemouth and then to Horsham where they spent only a few months of the summer of 1928. If he is right, then the Vivian family moved into Horsham only after the Beresfords had moved to Hitchin. But we are still left to wonder why Vivian suddenly chose Horsham to set up home.

Whatever the answers to these questions, the fact is that Vivian moved into Airlie House, in Richmond Road, sometime during

1929.[13] Kitty Vivian is not too clear on this period although she remembers that her mother, who was an enthusiastic bridge player, joined the local bridge club and that the home had several dogs and cats called Toby, Punch, and Minette, which they did not take with them when they moved to London. She also recalls that her father liked gardening as well as walking and, when the opportunity arose, he went sea-fishing.[14]

John Farquharson had worked well for Vivian during his absence in France. However, Vivian's magazine contributions had almost ceased, so far as current research shows. There were three short stories published in 1926, one in 1927, one in 1928 and none in 1929. But Farquharson had found a new book publisher for Vivian, and a very supportive publisher, in the firm of Ward Lock & Co. Starting in 1927 they would remain the main publisher of Vivian's books until 1942.

Ward Lock & Co had been established in 1854 from offices at 158 Fleet Street. By the 1920s they had moved to Warwick House in Paternoster Row, where many publishers, such as Hutchinson, had set up in business. Whether it was the firm's famous chairman, Douglas Lock, who first bought Vivian's work, we cannot be certain. It was in November 1926, that Douglas, a son of George Lock (d. 1891) the co-founder of the firm, died suddenly at his home in Hadley Wood. He was only fifty-six years old and popularly known to the staff of Ward Lock as the 'Chief'. According to Edward Liveing: 'He had the faculty of being interested in those who worked for him, and his kindness extended to their families. Indeed, in every relation of life, he radiated good will.'[15] His brothers, Wilfred and Leslie Lock, took over. From 1931 Wilfred would be sole chairman until his retirement in 1943. 'From a literary point of view the house under their direction kept clear of the main eddies and currents that swung prose and poetry into changing and conflicting courses during the inter-war years, since most of the fiction and verse which it issued was of a light and popular type.'

While Mrs Belloc Lowndes and Stephen McKenna could be said to be representative of the 'serious novelists' published by the firm,

Ward Lock's other authors read like a Who's Who of top selling genre fiction authors. Liveing says: 'In the realms of crime and detective stories it included among its writers several brilliant exponents of their craft, E. Phillips Oppenheim, Edgar Wallace and Leslie Charteris among them. The most popular and successful of its authors was Dornford Yates, who made his first appearance as a Ward Lock writer in the *Windsor Magazine*.' That was in 1911. But among other writers Liveing neglected to mention were Nigel Tranter, Harry Stephen Keeler, Horace Annesley Vachell, Winston Graham (creator of the 'Poldark' series of novels), Katharine Tynan, Max Pemberton, Stanley Weyman, Otwell Binns, 'Valentine' (Archibald Thomas Pechey, 1876–1961, who also produced 47 detective thrillers for Ward Lock under the name of 'Mark Cross') and, of course, E. Charles Vivian. They would later also be the reprint publishers for Sir Arthur Conan Doyle and Sir Henry Rider Haggard. Pechey (writing as 'Valentine'/'Mark Cross'), who was also represented by John Farquharson, was soon to become a friend of Vivian.

Douglas Lock's son, also Douglas Lock, who had joined the company in 1918, became Vivian's editor and remained so until 1942, when he was forced to retire from the firm, the year Vivian, significantly perhaps, left Ward Lock. For Vivian, it would be a profitable partnership while it lasted.

However, in 1926, Hodder & Stoughton had still two more books to publish. One was another fantasy under the Vivian name and the other was a Charles Cannell novel. *A King There Was,* published in May was another 'lost race' fantasy, being a direct sequel to *The Lady of the Terraces* and featuring the same character Felippe Guttierez who, this time, narrates the story. It has the same setting among the Caras in a lost valley of the Andean Mountains. *The Passionless Quest*, published in June, was more serious staple fare from 'Charles Cannell'.

The Forbidden Door was the first of Vivian's books to be published by Ward Lock, in September 1927. It was an adventure novel with a touch of fantasy set on an unnamed island off Malaya. In the hills of this mysterious island stands an ancient palace ruled over by Fleur

Delage, a woman with a curious past made into a human tigress by the fiendish cruelty of her husband. Maraquita Terry, Fleur's cousin, is staying with her but when a lawyer turns up with the news that Maraquita is heir to a large fortune, Fleur passes herself off as the heiress. Enter a couple of hard-up English adventurers, Alan Coulson and Josiah Drinkwater, who are imprisoned by Fleur who falls in love with Coulson. But Coulson is in love with Maraquita. The two men escape, rescue Maraquita, in a succession of feats breathlessly narrated, and stop the lawyer handing over the fortune to Fleur. It is then that Fleur resorts to ancient mystic knowledge by which she can open 'the forbidden door' and release a poison cloud to destroy her enemies. All is well and Coulson winds up marrying Maraquita but it is not clear whether Fleur is dead. This allowed Vivian to bring her back in a sequel *The Tale of Fleur* (1929) while Josiah Drinkwater also reappeared in *Woman Dominant* (1929).

It should be pointed out that Alan Coulson of *The Forbidden Door* is not really the Rex Coulson of Vivian's later '*Coulson adventure series*' which he wrote under the 'Jack Mann' pseudonym, although he is clearly a prototype.

The *Times Literary Supplement* found *The Forbidden Door* 'an engrossing and mysterious story.'[16] The critic of the *South Wales Argus* said it was 'Imaginative literature of a high order, and the reader is enthralled from the first page to the last. The story is of outstanding merit. The dialogue is racy and piquant, and the settings are redolent of that mysticism of the Far East which never fails to allure and delight.'[17] *The Northern Echo* agreed: 'A cleverly written and enthralling story of the East. It is a book without a dull page, and Mr Vivian has drawn some delightful characters. Exciting and enjoyable.'[18] *The Liverpool Echo* found it 'very, very good; stirring and adventurous.'[19]

The sales reflected Ward Lock's faith in their first Vivian venture. *The Forbidden Door* was issued in four different editions between 1927 and 1931. Vivian's retelling of *Robin Hood and his Merry Men* was published in the same month as *The Forbidden Door*. This, as we have already discussed, proved Vivian's most reprinted book.

Vivian's 1928 output shot up to four titles, three of them as Vivian and one as Charles Cannell, of which three of them were published by Ward Lock.

Man Alone, published in January, is again set in the islands off Malaya. So popular a setting was this for Vivian that one wonders whether he ever travelled there. As with his South American settings, his research is well done, and the assumption that Vivian must have travelled to these locations has caused some biographical entries to describe him as 'a British adventurer and traveller.'[20]

In *Man Alone*, Captain Stanley Field, former master of a tramp steamer trading in the Far East, is released from jail. It is said that he killed his wife's lover, Arnold Rawson. Arnold's brother, John Rawson, had tried to make it look like murder by hiding his brother's revolver but the jury had accepted his self-defence plea. But Field is now sick of the world and goes to live as a hermit on Ilahu. He has an odd collection of books with him. Haverlock Ellis' *Psychology of Sex*, Kant's *Critique of Pure Reason*, a set of George Borrow's travel books, and the works of John Milton.

A shipwreck drowns Stanley Field's estranged wife and brings five survivors to Field's island, including John Rawson and his daughter, Sybil. Enter a real villain named Courthaugh, who manages a copra business on a neighbouring island. Courthaugh murders Rawson, and Field has to fight Courthaugh to protect Sybil with a predictable ending. The *Times Literary Supplement* felt 'The story is well planned and interesting, but there are no very agreeable people.'[21] *John O'London's Weekly* felt it was 'an excellent story.'[22] while the *Bournemouth Graphic* observed: 'Mr Vivian is proving one of our most virile writers of the present day. Each succeeding work from his pen appears to grow in strength and in characterisation. His latest contribution is an example which for clear and expressive telling could not be easily beaten.'[23]

Nine Days, which he had finished in December, 1927, was issued in June, 1928. It was another dramatic tale set in the same area of the world. Vivian dedicated the novel to another friend and author, Eden Phillpotts, in the form of a poem.

> Master, whose many-sided art has limbed
> The heather-purple spaces of our west
> And opened to our sight the moorland ways,
> And set us, dreaming, on the misty crest
> Of tor or beacon, and to valley homes
> Taken us, marvelling at the art that drew
> Passion aflame, or tenderness alight,
> Or strength at work, or love at pains to strew
> Some path with blossoms; Let this gift, with us,
> Be as to Mentor from Telemachus.

Vivian was a personal friend of Phillpotts. How they met is not clear but Vivian had already dedicated his first major fantasy novel *City of Wonder* 'to Eden Phillpotts, my friend, from the author'. Therefore, their friendship began prior to 1923 and presumably during his journalist career. Phillpotts was being published by Hutchinson at this time. When Phillpotts (1862–1960) died at the age of 98, he had produced 250 books of a variety of subjects but is best remembered for his Devon novels. He also wrote many weird tales under the name Harrington Hext and produced not only weird fantasy but also delightful medieval fantasies of knights and dragons. But it is typical of Vivian's story that their first encounter remains a mystery. Kitty Vivian remembers that her father and mother used to visit their friend in Devon quite regularly during the 1930s.

The story of *Nine Days* starts with a yacht on the open sea chartered by Colonel Lynd and his wife. Vivian is using the name that he had often used as a pen name. The Lynds are engaged in rescuing their son, Adrian Lynd, from a French penal settlement at Noumea. Also on board is Veronica Lynd, Adrian's wife. They find a man swimming in the sea miles from shore. They rescue him, although it seems he does not want to be rescued. The man is called Smith; a mining engineer. On the day of his wedding, his bride was being driven to the church by her brother when their car crashed and both were killed. The shock causes Smith to give up on life. Stranded on the Aipuru peninsula, he decides to end it by swimming out to sea.

Colonel Lynd does not believe the man's story, thinking him a French spy attempting to thwart the rescue of his son. It turns out that Adrian Lynd is a wastrel and undeserving of rescue. In fact, it emerges that he was already married when he went through a marriage ceremony with Veronica. Smith forms a relationship with Veronica and participates in the rescue of Adrian who is shot and wounded during the escape. As the yacht attempts its getaway, it is stopped by a French destroyer. Smith gallantly volunteers to claim that he is Adrian Lynd to fool the French authorities. But Adrian, fortunately, dies of his wound and Smith's sacrifice is rendered unnecessary. Smith and Veronica leave the desolated colonel and his wife at Brisbane and head for a new life together.

The *Times Literary Supplement* felt it was 'a dramatic story'.[24] Eden Phillpotts wrote a critique for future editions of the work. '*Nine Days* seems to me to be a book providing everything that a distinguished novel can provide. There is wonderful, subtle humour, fine characterisation, atmosphere, rapid movement and an interesting plot—a fascinating plot.' The novel went to three editions between 1928 and 1931 and in September 1933, Ward Lock reissued it once more in their sixpenny paperback series.

The third Ward Lock publication of that year was *The Moon and Chelsea*. This was another 'serious' novel under the Charles Cannell by-line demonstrating, says Ward Lock's blurb, that Cannell was 'a brilliant writer of human romance'. The book was not particularly noted by critics although it went through three editions.

Vivian's fourth book that year was not published by Ward Lock. In fact it was a commission from Hurst and Blackett and was an adaptation of a screenplay, doubtless secured for Vivian by Farquharson. The film was a thriller entitled '*Shooting Stars*', with a story by Anthony Asquith (1902–1968) the director son of Lord Oxford. The film actually marked Asquith's debut as a director, albeit as co-director with A.V. Bramble, but Bramble acted simply as technical advisor. The twenty-five-year-old Asquith had not only written the story line of '*Shooting Stars*' but co-written the screenplay with J. O. C. Orton, who later became a regular supplier of scripts for Will Hay and the Crazy Gang. The original running time was 120 minutes. It was released in 1927.

Vivian's adaptation of *Shooting Stars* kept closely to the screenplay and enhanced it. Mary Prentiss Gordon, the screen star 'Mae Feather' (played by Annette Benson) is known in public as the wife of actor Julian Gordon (played by Brian Aherne). Both work for New Comet Film Corporation. But Mary is having an affair with slapstick comedian Andy Wilkes (Donald Calthrop). Andy has been offered an American contract and Mary wants to follow him. Julian threatens her with divorce and divorce will ruin her career.

Shooting a final scene for a film, an actor called Kellaway, has to chase Andy Wilkes and shoot him. The scene is all too real and while the director is congratulating the cast, they realise Andy has really been shot dead. Someone has put real bullets in the 'prop' gun. But the gun was to be used in a scene in which Julian Gordon is shot. The switch was only made at the last minute. Julian was the intended victim not Wilkes. The only person with access to the gun was Mary. Julian lies to divert suspicion from her so that he could punish her in his own way. He divorces her and ruins her career.

Six years later Julian, in charge of the New Comet Film Corporation, is now in love with Winnie Dobson (played by Chilli Bouchier). They are working on a film. The final scene is in a cathedral. Julian shouts for a woman extra to walk forward, kneel and pray before the altar. A dowdy woman is chosen, one Adeline Johnson, her face obscured by her hat. She does the scene. Julian does not recognise her. It is Mary Gordon, onetime star 'Mae Feather'. The scene is finished. The lights go out. She is left alone with Julian. But Julian is intent on his script and does not pay attention when she shuffles out. He wonders why the memory of Mary has come to his mind. Then he remembers Winnie is waiting for him.

Critic Geoff Brown felt 'the movie's pace is refreshingly lively...'[25] Certainly, it was a portend of greater things to come from the young Anthony Asquith.

Vivian did a proficient job of rendering Asquith's story and screenplay into a readable novel. Hurst and Blackett published in

October but, while the book was clearly a 'film tie-in' volume, the publishers did not even think it worthwhile to reproduce any still from the movie as illustration.

During his last year in France, Vivian produced two more novels that were to be his output for 1929. They were two sequels to his previous fantasy adventure *The Forbidden Door*.

The Tale of Fleur was published in February and features Fleur Delarge once more. The setting is still in a Dutch Protectorate in the East Indies. Fleur is using her charms on a local sultan, Abdul Ibn Farash Ibn Mulk, and an English sculptor, one Richard Grenville, employed by him. There is more melodrama than fantasy in the story and poison is dished out in liberal quantities with Fleur, who is truly in love with Grenville, making a grand exit by killing herself with a phial of exotic poison. Josiah Drinkwater, from the first novel, reappears, now running the Bhagava Grand Hotel. Drinkwater supplies some humorous touches. The *Times Literary Supplement* felt 'the chief merits are plenty of vigorous incident and freedom from morbid streaks often decried in fiction that deals with the Dutch East Indies.'[26] *The Daily Express* critic believed it 'a well written book. Told in a racy manner, and there is plenty of plot.'[27]

Josiah Drinkwater, now a deserter from a tramp steamer, makes a third appearance in *Woman Dominant*. This was published in July and went back to Vivian's 'lost race' fantasy theme. Furness and Quain are off down a tropical river when they are joined by Drinkwater. They are searching for a man and woman who disappeared twenty-five years before. The woman was Furness' mother and the man was her lover. It was Furness' own father who condemned them to be marooned in this part of the world. Once more the evil father appears in Vivian's fiction. And once more the evil father has a death-bed repentance and confesses all to his son who sets off to rescue his mother.

Drinkwater, Furness and Quain arrive in a strange country where the women drug their men, forcing the stupefied wretches to work in perpetual slavery. They discovered not only Furness' mother, still alive, but her daughter, Stephanie... the daughter of her lover.

Furness' love for his mother is somewhat tested and he reacts at his unexpected half-sister and seeks to run off, wrecking the launch. It is Drinkwater who is the hero and brings the party back from the land of dominant women. The *Times Literary Supplement* critic liked the novel: 'In all the fantasy there is no dullness.'[28] *The Sunday Referee* felt that 'the author has a fine sense of character and can create atmosphere swiftly and effectively. Good fun and a very readable novel.'[29] Ward Lock was able to produce three editions of it by 1932.

The theme of women giving men a mysterious powder which renders them fearful of the women and makes the women dominant, is, curiously, a theme which was picked by Gene Roddenberry, the creator of 'Star Trek'. In 1974 he made a television feature-length pilot for a projected series for Warner Brothers Television, called 'Planet Earth' and which stars John Saxon and Diana Muldaur. Roddenberry produced and wrote this idea by which a tribe of women had this mysterious drug. This is not to say that Roddenberry borrowed the idea directly from Vivian's novel. The concept came to be fairly widely used by fantasy writers at one time. But it is interesting that it has its roots in *Woman Dominant*.

By the time Vivian returned to England in 1929 it was difficult to disagree with the enthusiasm of the *Bournemouth Graphic* that 'Mr Vivian is proving one of our most virile writers of the present day'. It seemed that there were no clouds to mar Vivian's life.

However, within a few months of his return to England, an 'old friend' had re-appeared in the person of Mrs Lillian Simmons.

Notes

1. *The Times*, January 14, 1933.
2. Katharine Vivian Ashton, letter to author, September 1, 1990.
3. Katharine Vivian Ashton, letter to author, April 23, 1990.
4. Katharine Vivian Ashton, letter to author, March 14, 1994.
5. Elizabeth Beresford in conversation with author, June 10, 1994.
6. Jon Wynne-Tyson in conversation with author, June 10, 1994.

7. Katharine Vivian Ashton, letter to author, March 18, 1994.
8. Katharine Vivian Ashton, letter to author, October 12, 1992.
9. *Ibid.*
10. Katharine Vivian Ashton, letter to author, October 12, 1992.
11. Marcus Beresford (Mark Brandel) letter to Jack Adrian, May—1994.
12. Katharine Vivian Ashton, letter to author, January 28, 1994.
13. Katharine Vivian Ashton, letter to author, June 10, 1994.
14. *Ibid.*
15. *Adventure in Publishing: The House of Ward Lock 1854-1954*, Edward Liveing, Ward Lock & Co, London, 1954, p. 88/93.
16. *Times Literary Supplement*, October 20, 1927.
17. *South Wales Argus*, October 24, 1927.
18. *Northern Echo*, October 25, 1927.
19. *Liverpool Echo*, October 4, 1927.
20. Vivian's entry in *Who's Who in Horror and Fantasy Fiction*, Mike Ashley, Hamish Hamilton, London, 1977.
21. *Times Literary Supplement*, February 16, 1928.
22. *John O'London's Weekly*, February 10, 1928.
23. *Bournemouth Graphic*, March 2, 1928.
24. *Times Literary Supplement*, August 16. 1928.
25. BFM Review, *British National Film Catalogue*, 1975.
26. *Times Literary Supplement*, March 14, 1929.
27. *Daily Express*, February 28, 1929.
28. *Times Literary Supplement*, August 22, 1929.
29. *Sunday Referee*, August 11, 1929.

CHAPTER SEVEN

THE OLD BAILEY TRIAL

Kitty Vivian recalled living in Horsham from 1929 'until about 1931 or 1932, when we moved to London and lived first in Chelsea...'[1] Kitty's memory is, however, a few years out. Vivian and his wife, Marion, had moved to London sometime shortly before April, 1930. They moved into 29 Colville Terrace, W11, which was in North Kensington, though part of the Kensington and Chelsea borough.

It was in April that year that Vivian made a curious journey to Hadleigh, near Benfleet, in Essex. His father, James Henry Cannell, was dying. According to Kitty Vivian, her father had not seen or contacted his father since he had run away from home and changed his name in 1900. Now the 81-year-old Cannell 'ne'er-do-well' was reaching the end of his sad life. Numerous questions tumble through one's mind. Was there to be the deathbed repentance that Vivian had so often wrote about in his fiction? Did James Henry Cannell understand the trauma that he had put his son through? It is yet another mystery that we shall never know the answer to. All that is known are the facts that on April 26 at Magdala Castledane, Hadleigh, James Henry Cannell died of morbus cardis and syncope. Vivian, signing his original name as 'Charles H. Cannell', and firmly identifying himself as James Henry's son, with his London address, went to the local Rayleigh Register Office to register the death and to make the funeral arrangements.[2]

For thirty years he had been estranged from his father and poured out his frustrations in his fiction. Now his father was dead. It is hard to know what Vivian felt when, after the funeral of James Henry, he look the train back from Benfleet to his Chelsea home. Kitty Vivian cannot recall either having met her grandmother or grandfather. 'I never met his parents, and there was, I think, some sort of feud between them—I don't remember hearing anything about my grandfather's death.'[3]

Kitty had been nearly twelve years old when the family had returned to England. Almost immediately she was sent as a boarder to the Crofton Grange Girls' School in Orpington in Kent. Vivian obviously wanted a better education for his daughter than he, or his two sisters, had received. After leaving Crofton Grange, Kitty Vivian returned to France. The fact that she was away from home so much is doubtless the answer to her lack of knowledge of this traumatic time for her father.

Kitty does remember that her father liked France, in spite of the fact that even during the years they lived there, he had not learnt to speak French. Every year, after their return to England, Vivian would take Marion and Kitty back to France. They would head for the same place—Rotheneuf, near St Malo, on the northern coast of Brittany. It was then a small place of dunes, cliffs and pines. It boasted two beaches, the Plage du Val, open to the sea, and the Plage du Harve, an almost land-locked bay. On the headland stood the Hotel des Rochers Sculptes after the sculptured rocks along the coast, the work of Abbe Foure who began this work during the time of Vivian's visits and completed it in the 1950s, after twenty-five years. They first stayed at the Pension Bendeville on the cliff and then made the Grand Hotel opposite the Plage de Val their regular accommodation in the village. Kitty Vivian says he enjoyed Rotheneuf. 'Arriving at our hotel, he would soon make friends with anyone who looked like 'chum material', giving the holiday a good start. We bathed every day and my father was a good swimmer.'[4]

In 1931 Vivian's magazine output was down to one short story in the April edition of *Cassell's Magazine*. Ward Lock, however, were now happily producing an average of three Vivian novels a year. The three for 1930 were *Double or Quit* (January), *One Tropic Night* (May) and *Delicate Fiend* (July).

Double or Quit marked a departure for Vivian in that this was his first detective mystery in the traditional mould. A rich, grumpy old recluse named Wrench trusts only his manservant, Cobb. But Cobb forges his master's signature to a cheque, thinking it will not be discovered for some time. The forgery is soon detected and Wrench sends for the police. When the police arrive they find that Cobb has lost his head and tried to strangle Wrench. Cobb has fled, however, leaving the old man alive. Detective Sergeant Sydney Barr (the pseudonym Vivian had used in *Flying*) is confident that he will get his man. Time passes and Cobb has vanished. It now seems certain that someone must be shielding Cobb, although the evidence seems ridiculous, and things point to Wrench as the culprit. Chance reveals the extraordinary and gruesome truth behind the mystery. It was an excellent thriller and a foretaste of what was to come. The *Times Literary Supplement* was delighted with it. 'There is an excellent play to be found in this novel—the characters arrest attention and inspire sympathy, the action moves smoothly from one dramatic point to another, and the plot develops with fitting inevitability.'[5] Alas, no one took up the idea to dramatise the book either for the theatre or for the cinema.

In *One Tropic Night* Vivian returns once more to the tropical East for an adventure tale. The son of Yen Tsing Toi, a powerful Chinese businessman, is murdered on Mautate, a small island near the Malay Peninsula. The man who keeps a store on the island, one Bob Terry, kills the murderer. Yen Tsing Toi then arrives and wishes to reward Terry who declines any favour. Terry has, however, a daughter Patricia, educated in Kuala Lampur, and he has amassed some pearls for her future security. After his death, Patricia's uncle and cousin, having heard of the cache, plan to deprive her of it. This is known to Yen Tsing Toi who engages a young man named Tom Heron to watch over her and see that she comes into her own. After various adventures and misadventures, Heron confounds the wicked uncle and nephew, finds the pearls and wedding bells start sounding. The *Times Literary Supplement* was not particularly impressed[6] but the *Yorkshire Observer* felt it was 'A thrilling tale' with 'the tropical East vividly and dramatically depicted and the characters make a memorable impression.'[7]

With the third book *Delicate Fiend* (July), Vivian returned to the theme of crime mystery. Sir Roden Symons is a scientist, a leading authority on explosives and an amateur criminologist. He has been overworking and his doctor persuades him to go for a rest at Dr Violet Haslam's 'health farm', as we would call it nowadays. There are an odd assortment of people 'resting' there. Ida Karelia is an actress with a man-eating reputation. After a slow build up, Ida is found murdered in the grounds. The suspects are the guests. Inspector Ward arrives but it is Sir Roden who puts his energies into solving the murder, the culprit being none other than Dr Haslam herself, who, in fact, seems to have built up quite a score with three other deaths on her hands. Bill Haslam, Dr Haslam's nephew, and Sir Roden's niece, Greta Carden, provide the romantic interludes. Yet again the *Times Literary Supplement* was not overly impressed: 'This is a very readable story; but it fails in the attempt to combine romance, drama, mystery and tragedy.'[8] The critic of the *Morning Post* demurred: 'Really well done. Romance is alive as few mystery romances are.'[9]

The three novels published in 1931 included what was to be Vivian's last attempt at producing a Charles Cannell novel. However, Douglas Lock at Ward Lock refused to have anything more to do with Cannell. Cannell was not regarded as light enough for the list. Vivian's agent Farquharson was forced to find another publisher and did so in the person of John Lane, The Bodley Head. John Lane, The Bodley Head were certainly as 'up-market' as any author could get.

The last Cannell novel, *And the Devil*, is a strong novel, with undercurrents of a murder mystery. A maid, Gladys, comes down early one morning to prepare a house in Lancaster Gardens, W2, and finds the master of the house, thirty-two year old Cedric Walter

Harding, lying dead. The police are called as well as Stanley Adams, the family doctor. Cedric has taken poison. The whisky decanter nearby holds cyanide; is it murder? The murder mystery, for Vivian, was merely a literary device for a novel of social comment for we now explore the life of Cedric and his sister Aline. Dr Adams' had delivered them as babies and is able to trace their downward lifestyles. Cedric proceeds down the drinking, womanising and gambling route. A selfish, uncaring man, who ruins all he comes into contact with. Aline becomes a prostitute. As we reach the end of the novel we find that it is Dr Adams who is judge and jury on Cedric's lifestyle. 'If I saw any sign of usefulness in Cedric Harding, any possibility of his life proving a beneficial influence on any one person, I should not think of ending it in this way. But I see no such sign, no such possibility.' It is Dr Adams who has laced the decanter with cyanide. The *Times Literary Supplement* admitted 'although the subject is unpleasant, the forceful writing holds the attention.'[10] The book was reprinted by John Lane, The Bodley Head, two years later but no more Charles Cannell novels were ever written.

Unwashed Gods (January) came out under the Vivian name but was more reminiscent of Vivian at his most serious. It was as if the book should have appeared under the Cannell name with *And the Devil* appearing under the Vivian name. It was more of a 'serious novel' than *And the Devil*, and therefore Ward Lock's decision not to publish the Cannell volume but to opt for *Unwashed Gods* was a curious one. The 'unwashed gods' in question were, according to the *Times Literary Supplement*, 'that body of British workers who prefer to live in idleness on State aid rather than do an honest day's work. In contrast are the English gentlemen of the tale who compare the workers to a mob filled with collective brutality and selfishness.'[11] Vivian seems to have completely changed his attitudes to the labouring class, as expressed in his novel *The Young Man Absalom* (1915) when his hero was clearly supportive of Socialism and workers' rights.

Kitty Vivian confirms that during this period her father had two pet dislikes: David Lloyd George and Socialist politicians and ideas.

'He was not politically active in any way, but was strongly opposed to Socialist ideas.'[12]

In *Unwashed Gods*, behind the biased social commentary, we have a murder mystery. Set in a claustrophobic village atmosphere, Margaret Allen is thought to be so good that she could never do any wrong. But she is discovered not only pregnant by a mystery lover but she is then murdered. Suspicion falls on another woman: Miss Duquesne, owner of a large house and even larger fortune, who is thoroughly disliked by everyone. The villagers descend on her and are about to mete out their form of 'justice'. The real culprit turns out to be the village doctor who is the father of the dead Margaret's unborn child. As the *Times Literary Supplement* observes: 'The characters are not very real.'[13] However, the *Liverpool Post* thought it 'An ingenious story. The mystery—a good one—is skilfully handled, and there is enough incident to satisfy the most exacting.'[14]

Innocent Guilt (July) was very much a mystery thriller with a Svengali-like Ward Crowden, who has hypnotic powers and manages to persuade Hugh Derwent, a city magnate, to marry his daughter Theresa and so obtain control over the wealth firm of Derwent Brothers. Theresa realises that her father is mad and calls in the help of Richard Kaye, who, after various complex adventures, solves what turns out to be a mystery. The *Times Literary Supplement* felt 'The conversations are a little too facetious but the story is briskly told, and works up to an exciting climax.'[15] The *Northern Echo* was more enthusiastic: 'As a straight narrative without any highly involved plot, this is one of the best thrillers of the holiday season. It is a story which never flags in interest and the action moves with pleasing vigour.'[16]

In 1932 Ward Lock produced its usual three titles from Vivian. *Infamous Fame* (January), *Lone Isle* (May) and *False Truth* (September). In *Infamous Fame* old General Burne, the hero of El Aghred, receives an anonymous note referring to the events of twenty-six years before, of the battle in North Africa with which his fame rests. The old general realises that a man he thought had perished in the desert at El Ahgred is still alive and knows the truth of Burne's cowardice and treachery during that action. Instead of being a hero Burne is a liar and coward. The survivor reveals himself before a company of Burne's business associates. One of them, Stead, is in love with the general's daughter and tries to protect her father. But the general writes a suicide note and ends it all. Stead tries to stop the note falling into the girl's hand but it does. She forgives him and he retains her love. As usual during this period, the *Times Literary Supplement* was not too impressed[17] but the *Cambridge Daily News* observed: 'For gripping incidents, clear character sketching, delicious humour and stark tragedy, all the work of an artist, *Infamous Fame*, will take a lot of beating.'[18]

It was back to the Dutch East Indies for the second book *Lone Isle*. Two twin brothers, Edward and Oliver Stone bought four-fifths of a pearl fishery business from one Da Silva. One of the brothers went to live on the spot to oversee the business while the other remained a 'sleeping partner' in London. Sixteen years pass and no word has been received from Oliver in the East Indies although the dividends flowed back satisfactorily. A young man, Victor Wharton, sets out to clear up the mystery and finds his life threatened at every turn. Rita Stone, Edward's daughter, provides the romance. The denouement is not the least surprising feature of the tale. Vivian seems to have had a fan at *Cambridge Daily News* who enthused: 'Thrilling mystery, intriguing action, and a beautiful love story tinged with tragedy makes *Lone Isle* one of the best things the author has done.'[19]

The third book was a mystery thriller *False Truth*. Ercole, an exhibition dancer with an evil reputation, is shot dead in a card room of a third rate nightclub. Stanley Cosway, who had threatened to kill Ercole, had been in the club that night. He was sentenced to hang for the murder on circumstantial events. Cosway has a problem. He thinks he is protecting his wife and that she killed Ercole while Leone Cosway thinks her husband is really guilty. Bernard Holt, a young American friend of the defending counsel, conceives an admiration for Leone and works to establish Cosway's innocence. He discovers that Ercole was a blackmailer and was attempting to blackmail a drug trafficking gang. Leone is innocently involved. Holt smashes the gang, frees Leone and saves Cosway. The *Times Literary Supplement* observed: 'Cosway is a most unpleasant creature, who hardly seems worthy of the trouble of keeping alive to be a barrier between Holt and Leone. In fact, he is too unpleasant to live, and it is his own uncontrollable temper that kills him when he accuses Leone of being Holt's mistress.'[20] The *Medical Times* believed *False Truth* to be 'One of the best entertaining novels we have read for a long time. This brilliant writer has excelled himself in writing it.'[21]

Perhaps there was one signed copy of *False Truth* Vivian would come to regret presenting. He gave a copy to his mistress, Lillian Simmons. The inscription read: 'Dear Babs, wishing you good.' But during 1932 the relationship was distinctly cooling. In 1930 Vivian was visiting Lillian in her home in Fort Road, Bermondsey, and had been given a key, going only when he knew her husband was at work. It is now, according to Vivian, that she suddenly demanded money from him to stop her husband citing him as co-respondent in divorce proceedings. There is no denying that Vivian was having an affair with Lillian Simmons but, according to Vivian, she was now attempting to blackmail him because he had ended the relationship when he found out she had another lover.

Vivian went to the police after Lillian sent a friend to demand £250 from him. This was Claude William Neale, a motor coach drive with whom she was also having an affair. On police advice, Vivian arranged to meet Lillian Simmons on December 8 1932, and gave her a cheque for £100. As soon as she accepted the cheque, the police arrested her and she was charged with 'demanding £250 with menaces'. However, the case was brought as a private prosecution on behalf of Vivian. The trial opened at the Central Criminal Court on Thursday, January 14 1933. The trial judge was Sir Ernest Wild KC, the Recorder of London. This might have given Vivian some pause for thought, for Wild (1869–1934) was known for expressing a dislike of writers of mystery stories. In 1929, according to the *Illustrated Police News*, he had sentenced a 19-year-old musician to three months imprisonment and twelve strokes of the birch for trying to rob a jewellery store having, his defence counsel stated, his mind filled with crime stories. 'Is it an excuse for crime?' thundered Sir

Ernest. He was a notorious 'flogging judge' who frequently gave out sentences involving birching concurrent with imprisonment. Sir Ernest's average flogging orders with the birch was between twelve and twenty strokes.

Prosecuting the case against Lillian Simmons, who pleaded 'not guilty' to the charge, was Geoffrey Darling Roberts, later a KC and OBE. During the proceedings, Vivian was given anonymity as 'Mr V'. Roberts opened the case with Vivian's admission of the facts of his affair going back to 1924. In late 1932, Lillian had told Vivian that her husband was instituting divorce proceedings naming Vivian as correspondent but told him she would get her husband to stop the proceedings if Vivian gave her £250. If he did not pay, she would inform Marion Vivian of her husband's infidelity. Vivian admitted giving her two amounts of £30 and £20. Vivian asserted that he owed the woman nothing.

Defending Lillian Simmons was a leading defence counsel, St John (Jack) Hutchinson KC (1884–1942). Hutchinson and his wife Mary Barnes mixed in the world of high literature and art. Mary had been mistress to the critic Clive Bell (1881–1964) of The Bloomsbury Set. Hutchinson was not known for charity work so one also questions how the wife of a £4 a week council clerk would guarantee the fee of such a distinguish counsel. She had been on bail since her arrest. The question of who stood bail also occurs, although the exact sum is not recorded in the surviving reports.[22] After the prosecution had put their case, the court was adjourned until Monday, January 17. Lillian Simmons' defence was the story of a young woman, albeit recently married, impressed by the older Vivian, a famous author, who befriended her and began to ask her for money which she was apparently able to give him. Pressed by counsel, she admitted the relationship was an 'intimate one'. She said the affair went on from 1924 to 1928, the years that Vivian was living in Paris and St Jean-de-Luz, in the south of France. Curiously, the mechanics of how that was possible with Lillian in Bermondsey and Vivian in Paris, and later the south of France, does not seem to have been questioned. Vivian himself had admitted the affair.

During this time, Lillian said she had given Vivian £66 in 1925, and in 1926 had given him £50 and a further £40 after pawning her jewels and her husband's gold chain, without her husband's knowledge.

Lillian Simmons told the story of how the relationship was renewed in 1930 and how Vivian had a key to her house in Fort Road, Bermondsey. He would visit when her husband was at work. Visiting her in October 1931, he found she had kept his letters to her and was 'cross' and ordered them to be destroyed. She told the court she had 60 letters and burned them. She added that in the drawer, with the letters, were ten £1 notes and Vivian said he was hard up and so she let him have the money.[23]

At this time, Vivian, she said, told her that he had a play called 'Untitled' that was going to be produced with Fay Compton and Robert Courtneidge and would pay her back with interest. She pawned her piano and her sewing machine to give him more money.

One wonders why her husband did not ask about the disappearance of his gold chain, the piano or sewing machine from their small apartment. At least counsel sought the answer and Lillian Simmons replied that her husband did ask and she put him off by telling him that she had invested the money in an underclothing business. She said that Vivian had repaid her £20 in May 1932 and when she asked for more, bringing up the idea that her husband was going to divorce her and name Vivian as co-respondent, Vivian agreed but wanted her to sign an agreement in which the word 'blackmail' was used.

In November 1932, Lillian Simmons admitted that she had sent a friend, Claude William Neate to see Vivian and demand £250. Cross-examined by Vivian's counsel, Lillian Simmons admitted that she was also having an affair with Neate, who worked for a motor coach company, and was married but living apart from his wife. She further admitted that she went to an inn in Buckinghamshire where she and Neate shared a room. On a subsequent occasion 'she was there on *business* with Mr Neate and "Mr V".' A chance remark by the landlady about the room alerted Vivian to the fact that she was not just having an affair with him, and Vivian told her the affair was off. Questioned by counsel about her husband's threat of naming Vivian in divorce proceedings, which she would stop for £250, Lillian Simmons claimed that she had never mentioned this to Vivian.[24] Certainly, as Vivian's counsel had said in his opening, a search had been made of Divorce Court records and no such proceedings were pending.

The most extraordinary witness was Lillian's husband, Clarence George Simmons, who told the court that he had known nothing about his wife's relationship with Vivian, nor it seems with Claude Neate, or her trips to the inn in Buckinghamshire, until his wife was arrested before the trial. While he said that he and Lillian lived in an eight shilling a week rented flat in Fort Road, Lillian had already told the court that it was a six room house. Simmons said that he had managed to save about £150 over the years, which had all gone (not the £250 that his wife claimed she had lent to Vivian). He added that his wife did not seem extravagant and that he trusted her.

The defence counsel asked, 'And you have forgiven her?'

'I have forgiven her,' replied the tearful Mr Simmons.

The evidence being concluded, it was a matter of whether the jury believed Vivian or Lillian Simmons. Sir Ernest put the matter this way—asking the jury if they thought it would not be safe to convict on the evidence before them. After consulting among themselves, the foreman replied: 'We do.'

'Do you substantially believe Mrs Simmons story?'

'Yes.'

'It follows that you disbelieve "Mr. V.".'

The foreman agreed.

'So do I,' said Sir Ernest.

That meant a 'Not Guilty' verdict and the defence counsel immediately asked that the prosecution pay the costs.

Sir Ernest replied: 'I don't think I have the power to do that, but I have great satisfaction in depriving Mr Evelyn Charles Vivian, author, of his costs. He need no longer be under the cloak of anonymity.'

Thus, dramatically, as *The News of the World* stated, '"Mr V's" identity was revealed.'

Sir Ernest turned to the jury again.

'You believe he is lying?' he pressed again.

'Absolutely and entirely,' confirmed the foreman.

Sir Ernest went further: 'His story is one continuous and concocted lie. He has lived on this woman's bounty, and although she foolishly destroyed most of his letters, others consist of whining for money. He would not pay. He knew he ran the risk of being county-courted and he concocted this wicked story of blackmail. That is the view I take and, I take it, the view you take.'

'Yes,' agreed the foreman.

Sir Ernest then turned on Lillian Simmons. 'You leave this Court, with regard to this matter, without the slightest stain on your character... You go home and behave properly to your husband. Remember he has behaved well to you.'[25]

It seemed an extraordinary thing to say, even, if cleared of blackmail of Vivian Lillian Simmons had confessed in court to two adulterous affairs, and admitted to taking large sums of money from her husband's savings without his knowledge, pawning his possessions as well as their piano and her sewing machine to raise money. Yet Sir Ernest saw no cause to offer censure on her conduct. His full rancour was reserved for Vivian, and that rancour overlooked the fact that he was accepting the contents of the letters Lillian Simmons said she had destroyed were from Vivian asking for money. Sir Ernest added an important derogatory word, 'whining', allowing *The News of the World* to use 'Letters to a Woman Whining for Money' as a headline.

'In my view it was a wickedly concocted story. I shall retain the papers to consider whether I shall send them to the Public Prosecutor with a view of this considering a prosecution for perjury against Evelyn Charles Vivian.'

'Lillian Simmons was smiling through her tears and left the court with her husband,' observed *The News of the World* reporter.

The News of the World splashed their report once Vivian's identity was revealed by the judge: 'Wickedly Concocted Story of Blackmail', 'Judge's Stern Criticism of Author's Conduct', 'Married Woman Acquitted', 'Papers Impounded', 'Dramatic Revelation of "Mr. V's"

Identity' and 'Letters to a Woman Whining for Money'. *The Times* and the *Daily Telegraph* were more restrained.[26]

Alas, Kitty Vivian never referred to the case and so we will never know how Vivian reacted emotionally. It was a strange case which, from the evidence given in court, showed Lillian Simmons' character, by her own admission, as certainly questionable. While Vivian was willing to admit having a long-term relationship with her, why would he demand money from her after her sexual favours? The excuses of needing money to go to Paris, and money to back two plays he had written does not ring true. By the time of the trial he had published 47 books, many of them sold very well indeed, and he had achieved a considerable reputation. By then his short stories and serials had appeared in most of the top UK magazines and newspapers. Reading the available evidence there is in my mind several questions which arise and a feeling that here is an example of an unsafe verdict.

Immediately following the trial, significantly, he took a cruise by himself to the Near East. His daughter phrased it this way: 'He went once, alone, on a cruise to the Near East from which he obtained material for the Coulson and Gees books.' It has been impossible to ascertain whether Sir Ernest Wild, who died in the following year 1934, put through the request to the Public Prosecutor's Office to pursue Vivian for perjury, whether the application was refused or, indeed, whether this curious verdict was ever challenged. In the circumstances, one certainly cannot blame Vivian for deciding to drop out of sight on a lengthy cruise for awhile.

The end of the trial did throw up an interesting piece of information. *The Times* carried a short item under the heading 'Mr. Charles Vivian'.

'Mr Charles Vivian, author and journalist, of 3 Hare Court, Temple, EC4, wishes it made clear that he is not the same person as the Mr Evelyn Charles Vivian, an author, who at the Central Criminal Court on Monday was disclosed as the prosecutor ("Mr V") on a charge of blackmail. The accused woman was *Acquitted.*' [27]

The same item was carried by *The News of the World*, January 22 1933. This was a fascinating piece of information, as many had confused the two Vivians. Charles Vivian ensured that he had an entry in the *Writer's Who's Who* for 1934. He had been assistant editor of *Pearson's Magazine* 1910–12, then editor of *Novel Magazine* from 1912–22, *Cassell's Magazine* from 1922–24 becoming publicity press liaison officer for the British Empire Exhibition of 1924–25, and was then managing editor of *The London Weekly*. He was admired by novelist Ursula Bloom and recounted how she was awed to see his name on the door when she passed down a corridor in the Pearson building in 1919.[28]

After the cruise, Vivian did return to his wife, Marion, at 6 Callow Street, Chelsea. They then moved to 6 Manor Studios, 165a King's Road, SW3. He remained there until 1936 when they moved to a large apartment at 3a Longridge Road. He was to remain there with Marion and Kitty until a German incendiary bomb in 1941 drove them into temporary accommodation. Kitty said that the bomb had also destroyed all her father's papers and books.[29]

Yet personal and international gloom and doom apart, the year 1933 was to be one of importance for Vivian's writing career. It was to see the birth of his 'Jack Mann' stories and the same year saw the first appearance of Detective Inspector Terry Byrne of Scotland Yard. Although, almost immediately, Byrne was to be overshadowed in 1934 by a new and more powerful character, Inspector Jeremy Head of Westingborough, who was stated to be a cousin of Byrne and with Byrne having cameo roles in several of the Head novels.

Notes

[1.] Katharine Vivian Ashton, letter to author, September 1, 1990.
[2.] Information from death certificate & etc., St Catharine's House, London.
[3.] Katharine Vivian Ashton, February 14, 1994.
[4.] June 10, 1994.
[5.] *Times Literary Supplement*, February 20, 1930.
[6.] *Times Literary Supplement*, June 19, 1930.

7. *Yorkshire Observer*, June 20, 1930.
8. *Times Literary Supplement*, August 14, 1940.
9. *Morning Post*, December 10, 1931.
10. *Times Literary Supplement*, February 26, 1931.
11. *Ibid.*
12. Katharine Vivian Ashton to author, June 10, 1994.
13. *Times Literary Supplement*, February 26, 1931.
14. *Liverpool Post*, February 21, 1931.
15. *Times Literary Supplement*, September 10, 1931.
16. *Northern Echo*, September 11, 1931.
17. *Times Literary Supplement*, February 25, 1932.
18. *Cambridge Daily News*, January 28, 1932.
19. *Cambridge Daily News*, May 30, 1932.
20. *Times Literary Supplement*, February 9, 1933.
21. *Medical Times*, February 8, 1933.
22. *The Times*, January 14, 1933.
23. *The Times*, January 17, 1933 and *Daily Telegraph*. January 18, 1933.
24. *The News of the World*, January 22, 1933.
25. *The News of the World* (above) gave the most detailed account.
26. *The Times*, January 17, 1933, The Daily Telegraph, January 18, 1933.
27. *The Times*, January 18, 1933.
28. *The Mightier Sword*, Ursula Bloom, Robert Hale, London, 1966. p.22.
29. Katharine Vivian Ashton, to author September 1, 1990.

CHAPTER EIGHT

INSPECTOR BYRNE AND OTHERS

Detective Inspector Terence Herbert Byrne of Scotland Yard is a tall, thin, melancholy-looking man with appealing dark, soulful eyes. In fact, he is described more than once as looking as if he were 'a poet on the dole' rather than a detective. The curious thing about Byrne is that in all the various books in which he appears, including his cameo appearances in several of the Inspector Head mysteries, Byrne never takes a leading role. He is never the hero nor does he ever get the girl. Apart from the Inspector Head stories, where he is overshadowed by his country cousin, he appears in seven novels. We inevitably find him as an off-stage chorus to the amateur sleuth who is the hero. In no way did Vivian go out of his way to create a 'series hero' in Byrne as he did with Head, or as with Coulson or Gees in his 'Jack Mann' novels.

Byrne makes his initial appearance in *The Keys of the Flat* (January 1933). Sir Arthur Endliss is a leading analytical chemist who, therefore, has access to various poisons. Dione Bourne works as a secretary in his office. The suspicions of the police are aroused when Dione's friend, Erica 'Bunny' Adams, dies of arsenic poisoning within a few hours of eating a meal with her. A large quantity of arsenic is found mixed in the sugar in Dione's apartment. Dione does not take sugar but 'Bunny' did. Sir Arthur believes in his secretary's innocence and takes an interest in the case. But Dione is discovered to be the mistress of Peter Ashton, who has the key to her flat, and has also been pursuing 'Bunny'. Did Dione seek revenge on her friend or did Ashton want to get rid of Dione to have a clear field with 'Bunny'? In fact, neither motives are right, and both Ashton and Dione are innocent. With Byrne in support and Arthur Endliss on the trail, the mystery reaches a surprising climax, although, as the *Times Literary Supplement* says in retrospect, 'the one answer to all the various points of the puzzle was quite simple and obvious. A well-thought out and constructed thriller.'[1] Indeed, in *The Keys of the Flat* Vivian produced a classic 'whodunnit' and proved himself a master of the format.

When *Ladies in the Case* was published in April 1933, the *Times Literary Supplement* continued to be appreciative. 'There are very few writers of detective fiction who can defuse or disentangle a complicated story with the very persuasive confidence which characterises Mr Vivian's work. His latest thriller is neat in construction, difficult to anticipate and satisfying in solution.[2]

In this tale, one Alfred Blotz is trying to fence the Lienbaum Necklace, which 'Spider' Tuson has 'acquired' for him. But an adventuress named Lady Connie filches it from Blotz, whereupon Tuson pushes his luckless fence under a lorry, believing Blotz has tried to 'con' him. Dying, Blotz tells the story to his barrister Everard Thurston who promises to bring Lady Connie and Tuson to justice. The problem is, when Thurston and his friend Tom Maxwell start to investigate, they find that the Lienbaum Necklace has never been stolen in the first place. Behind this apparent contradiction is a tangle of interrelated plots, which gradually unravel to form the noose which convicts Tuson.

Later, in the 1930s, when Vivian had acquired the services of an American agent Otis Kline, Kline sold the book to T.V. Boardman & Co, New York, who published a US edition in 1942.

In *Girl in the Dark* (September 1933), Vivian returned Inspector Byrne as the investigator with the assistance of Sir Arthur Endliss and his secretary Dione Bourne from *The Keys of the Flat*. At the end of this novel Dione and Sir Arthur decide to get married. Byrne not only appears in the first 'Inspector Head' novel, *Shadow on the House*

(1934), but there are appearances by both Sir Arthur Endliss and Dione Bourne, now Lady Endliss

Girl in the Dark was dedicated to Vivian's American friend and colleague Harry Stephen Keeler 'who has done more toward lifting the mystery story from the domain of mere craftsmanship to that of artistic achievement than any other American author'. It appears likely that Vivian had first encountered Keeler's novels while a Hutchinson editor, and it is interesting that Keeler was published by Hutchinson while Vivian was there, but after Vivian joined Ward Lock Keeler, too, appeared on the Ward Lock list.

Keeler was editor of *10-Story Book*, which published Dashiell Hammett's very first story and which is now highly regarded by aficionados. Keeler had most of his books published in England first. His first novel was *The Voice of the Seven Sparrows*, published by Hutchinson in 1924 and it could be that Vivian was instrumental in persuading Hutchinson to publish it by reading it in manuscript first. He certainly became an enthusiastic supporter of Keeler who had 56 titles published plus four as joint author with his wife Helen Goodwin Keeler. Perhaps his best-known thriller was *The Spectacles of Mr Cagliostro* (Hutchinson, 1926) which was republished by Ward Lock in 1931 as *The Spectacles*.

Keeler himself dedicated two of his own books to Vivian. *The Defrauded Yeggman* (E.P. Dutton, 1937) was 'to my friend E. Charles Vivian of London' and in *10 Hours* (E.P. Dutton, 1937) the dedication ran 'This novel is dedicated to a British author who has written over fifty books, all of which I have read and enjoyed— E. Charles Vivian'.

In 1938 Vivian as 'Jack Mann' also dedicated *Maker of Shadows* 'To Harry Stephen Keeler because he turned the craft of mystery story writing into art'. The admiration Vivian has for Keeler is also demonstrated by the fact that Gees' secretary in *Gees First Case* is reading a Keeler novel.

'He got off the corner of the desk. "What are you reading?" he added.

'"One of Keeler's." She held it up.

'"Ah! Clever chap, Harry S.K. Always manages to get the human touch, somehow."'[3]

In *Girl in the Dark* Cuthbert Ellis is a trustee of a Will for two young people: his niece Isabel Carr and Hugh Colvin, and has gambled with the money which was not his own. He is suspected of the murder of the second trustee. Isabel is convinced of his guilt and she joins forces with Hugh Colvin, thwarting a plan to kill Hugh. The ending is a surprise one and features an ingenious method of killing. Rather than it being the butler who did it, it is the good-looking housekeeper who could blow poison darts through a hollow brass stair rail![4]

In April 1934, Ward Lock issued *Jewels Go Back*. The *Times Literary Supplement* said 'Very vivid and merciless is this picture of a man who rose from poverty to great wealth, got himself entangled with an insane wife, and then married again while the first wife was still alive in a lunatic asylum.'[5] Madeleine Catterwell does not realise her husband has an insane wife and a criminal son. The son turns up and threatens to expose his father and Catterwell shoots him. He tries to cover up the murder by making it look like a burglary, claiming he shot in self-defence. The *Times Literary Supplement* commended Vivian as 'the tale develops into a simple and moving account of the struggle of conscience at work'. Catterwell attempts to save Madeleine and his daughter from exposure of his previous life and crime. Oliver Carey, staying with the Catterwells, has fallen in love with Madeleine and it is he who discovers the secret. Tragedies follow. Catterwell loses his daughter in a bathing accident, while the police, not contented with the coroner's verdict of 'justifiable homicide', learn the truth of the crime. Catterwell commits suicide.

The Capsule Mystery (June 1935) starts with Hector Aland, managing director of Odile de Sevigne, Bow Street, beauty specialists, entertaining his friend Mrs Edith Sinclair. Mrs Sinclair is more than a friend; she is Aland's mistress and has set him up in business. It is clear that Aland is tired of her. Aland has been taking some capsules for a cold, a mixture of cinnamon and quinine tablets made by a reputable chemist. Mrs Sinclair asks for one, the last in the box which he then throws on the fire. She takes the capsule, collapses and is dead. A doctor pronounces it poisoning by cyanide. Aland is recognised as Hector Alan Dunn who has served a prison sentence for City fraud. The police arrest him for murder. He is tried but acquitted for the defence's investigation leads to the actual murderer.[6]

The Impossible Crime, published in January 1940, was not entirely liked by the *Times Literary Supplement* reviewer. 'The novel opens excitingly and the policemen are well drawn but the romance is embarrassing and the detective grows tedious. Mr Vivian has done better.'[7] It is a little too harsh a judgment. A butler is found hanged after an attempted burglary in the house of his wealthy employer. The burglar is clearly not the murderer, however, and it is fairly easy for the discerning reader to see who it is. Therefore, readers are not allowed to reach any solution but have to observe the workings of the somewhat ponderous police machine through their investigation.

Inspector Byrne returned in fine fettle in *Man With a Scar*, published in September 1940. In this book we are back to the old Vivian high standard of entertainment. *Man With a Scar* is one of Vivian's best mystery thrillers. Lawyer Richard Stanton is down on his luck. The girl he was deeply in love with has died eight months prior to the opening of the book. His life is shattered. He has lost his job and purpose for living. He has no money but has acquired a 'couple of pills'. He decides to go to Valli's for one last meal, for which he cannot pay, but plans to take the pills to swallow with his coffee and make an exit on life. This dramatic opening is full of colour and tension.

The man at the next table, a man with a scar, deliberately knocks over his cup with the poison. He has assessed Stanton's desperate plight and offers him £50, £20 immediately, to go to someone's flat and pick up some papers. Stanton finds the task not an easy one for there is a dead girl in the flat and outside, keeping watch, are two professional thugs.

The papers turn out to be a letter addressed to Aida Forester. Stanton decides not to claim the rest of his money but contacts Aida.

He is then plunged into a dangerous adventure, and romance blossoms, as he fights to save a bequeathed fortune for Aida against the machinations of those mysterious persons who want to cheat her of it. Stanton, with some off stage support from Byrne, solves the mystery and wins the girl in this very readable tale.

And Then There Was One, published in March 1941, was to be the last Vivian thriller published by Ward Lock. It was to be, in the parlance of the times, a veritable 'corker'. A number of people about to inherit fortunes from a trust are being murdered so simply and skilfully that the police gain our sympathy in their inability to deal with the crimes. The man who is next on the list seeks assistance from Inspector Terry Byrne. But again, Byrne plays second fiddle to a youthful hero, Maurice Delaney West, an estate agent, who gets involved because of his attachment for Margaret Curtis. The *Times Literary Supplement* was unduly enthusiastic about it. 'An exciting tale... One might argue from this, perhaps, that Mr Vivian himself belongs to Scotland Yard, a compliment he deserves by his able handling of detectives. Nevertheless, his hero is outside the Force, and it is he who proves the ablest at prevention (of the murders). The climax is, without any tricks of terror, hair-raising.[8]

It was a high note on which Vivian was to part company from Ward Lock. Indeed, this was to be the last Vivian novel to be published from Ward Lock. However, Inspector Byrne was to surface in three more novels, published by his new publisher Robert Hale— *Curses Come Home* (1942), *She Who Will Not* (1945) and the posthumous *Vain Escape* (1952).

It would appear that Byrne had rather a unique role in detective fiction, being the only detective who features in nearly a dozen books but never as the hero, or even the person who solves all the mysteries.

Notes

1. *Times Literary Supplement*, February 16, 1933.
2. *Times Literary Supplement*, June 8, 1933.

3. *Gees First Case*, by Jack Mann, Wright and Brown, 1936, p 39.
4. *Times Literary Supplement*, October 19, 1933.
5. *Times Literary Supplement*, May 31, 1934.
6. *Times Literary Supplement*, June 20, 1935.
7. *Times Literary Supplement*, June 27, 1940.
8. *Times Literary Supplement*, February 8, 1941.

CHAPTER NINE

'JACK MANN'

Although it had been known to his American readership that 'Jack Mann' was a pseudonym of E. Charles Vivian from as far back as 1950, it was not until W. O. G. Lofts, in his *Armchair Detective* article 'On the Trail of the Mysterious Jack Mann' (1972) that the British public came to appreciate the identity of the man who 'wrote brilliant mystery, fantasy and supernatural stories'.[1]

While Lofts' article contained numerous errors of fact, even to the dating of the first publication of some of the Mann books, it allowed Mike Ashley to properly identify Mann in his *Who's Who in Horror and Fantasy Fiction* (London, 1977), and later Donald H. Tuck to do so in his three volume study *The Encyclopedia of Science Fiction and Fantasy* (Chicago, 1978). But Mann had already been clearly identified as Vivian in the April 1950 issue of *A. Merritt's Fantasy Magazine*.

Even from 1950 there had been continued speculation among aficionados of the genre that 'Jack Mann' was really a brother of Vivian and that the two brothers probably worked in collaboration. It was, of course, not realised that Vivian had no brother.

The mystery of 'Jack Mann' is typical of the many mysteries which surround Vivian's life, and which cannot be explained by his daughter Kitty Vivian. But she felt that not even Vivian's agent John Farquharson knew that Vivian was writing as 'Jack Mann'. As Lofts commented, in praising Mann's brilliant fantasy tales, 'surely even he could not have spun such a web of mystery as that which surrounds his own identity!'[2] The truth is that Vivian was responsible for the many shadows that surround his life and more shadows were created by his daughter. To use the title of one of his 'Jack Mann' novels, he was a veritable 'Maker of Shadows'.

In 1932, Vivian was producing three novels a year for Ward Lock but doing very little magazine work. He obviously felt himself capable of greater efforts but Ward Lock were not interested in producing new Charles Cannell novels. However, in 1935 and 1936, David Lock did agree to republish two Cannell novels, which were more in the adventure style of Vivian. Ward Lock reissued these under the E. Charles Vivian by-line. These were *The Guardian of the Cup* (March 1935) and *Barker's Drift* (February 1936).

Vivian decided to start a new adventure series around a single character. He chose a merchant navy officer whom he called Rex Coulson. He had used Alan Coulson as a name in *The Forbidden Door* (1927) but Rex Coulson was to be made of sterner stuff.

His first book in the series was entitled *Reckless Coulson* and it seemed a much faster paced story than he usually wrote. Several murders, each following swiftly, a mysterious train hold-up by Chinese bandits against a fight for the possession of North China by local warlords, give a background for Rex Coulson on shore leave from his ship. He meets up with a revolutionary adventuress, Thelma Tsarkaya, who is instrumental in saving his life but involving him in all kinds of unpleasant raids and plots. She is diabolically attractive and ambitious, and causes Coulson a few moments of weakness before he discovers the leader of the bandits and, without seriously committing himself to Thelma, returns to a quieter life on shipboard.

Vivian decided to use the pseudonym 'Jack Mann' and apparently took the book to another agent. This agent, whose name Vivian's daughter could not recall, decided to take the manuscript to the firm of Wright and Brown. The company was run by two partners, from offices in Farringdon Avenue, just off Fleet Street. The firm specialised in popular fiction, their editions were sold primarily to lending libraries with secondary sales going to the general book buying public. *Reckless Coulson* was published in January 1933, and the talented 'Jack Mann' was immediately noticed. The *Times Literary Supplement* exclaimed: 'Innumerable thrills are here... Coulson is not at all the hackneyed adventurer of fiction, but a well-drawn figure, whose scheming leads him through a maze of difficulties to a thoroughly ingenious and satisfactory conclusion.'[3]

Between 1933 and 1942 'Jack Mann' was to produce fourteen titles for Wright and Brown. Of these titles the first six were devoted to the adventures of Rex Coulson. When Bill Lofts approached John Farquharson, Vivian's agent, while researching his article, Farquharson admitted that he had no knowledge that Vivian was turning out the 'Jack Mann' thrillers.

The second Coulson book followed hot on the heels of the first in September of 1933. This was *Coulson Goes South*, which adventure there is a touch of the Vivian 'lost race' theme with an African tribe claiming direct descent from ancient Atlantis. The story starts off with a similar idea to Vivian's *Woman Dominant*. Ten years have elapsed since Bernard Keyes and his son have been captured by 'the Sons of Yarab', dwelling in the inaccessible interior of the Sahara. Bernard's brother, Albert, discovers they are still alive and sets off to rescue them. He encounters Coulson who agrees, reluctantly, to join in the desperate venture. Coulson enters the stronghold of 'the sons of Yarab' alone, with hairbreadth escapes a romantic encounter without the conventional conclusion, and he successfully rescues Bernard and his son. The *Times Literary Supplement* still approved of 'Jack Mann'. 'A vigorous adventure story written with careful attention to detail.'[4] The *English Catalogue of Books* of 1941 lists a title *Coulson Goes North* as being in its 3rd reprint, in June 1936, at 3s. 6d.[5] No such book was published and it is clear that this must be regarded as a misprint for *Coulson Goes South*.

The Dead Man's Chest, published in January 1934, was the next Coulson adventure. In spite of the scarcity of this volume, Wright and Brown had issued it in three different editions while Godwin of New York published a concurrent American edition. Published in the same month came *Egyptian Nights*. Coulson and his ship are in

Alexandria and encounters the Russian adventuress, Thelma Tsarkaya, again. This time we have drug smugglers to deal with. But there was a new critic on the *Times Literary Supplement* who took an instant dislike to Coulson.

'The hero has had apparently previous adventures and is likely to have more for the ending is inconclusive. The author has noted the methods of drug smuggling as reported from time to time, but nothing else in the book has any touch of verisimilitude. The characters are not only unreal as types, but the author's poverty of invention forces them to act without rhyme or reasons; nor has the conversations any charm or humour. Those to whom this type of story appeals may be blind to inaccuracies of detail, but surely any writer should strive to avoid these.'[6]

When *Detective Coulson* was published in June 1935, it received a much more enthusiastic notice in the *Times Literary Supplement*: 'Bubbles over with zest and vitality... The proportion of deduction to excitement is well-balanced and, although there are some conventional features to the tale, the handling is brisk and agile.[7] Presumably, the more jaundice critic had departed to write his own novel. Coulson this time receives a message from a ship known to have been sunk eighteen months before. It involves him in a struggle for recovering secret naval plans and opposition from the espionage system of a foreign power. The *Times Literary Supplement* believed it to have 'an ingenious and exciting plot.'[8]

The last Coulson title, *Coulson Alone*, came out in April 1936. In this story Vivian returned to a favourite location, the East Indies. A wreck with 400 tons of tin lies on a reef, somewhere Java way. 'The Aspasia', of which Coulson is first officer, is chartered to salvage it. On board is Coulson's old romantic adversary, Thelma Tsarkaya, who has been commissioned to fetch four *Iguanodons* preserved in oil, like Siberian mammoths in ice, from an island near the reef. A villain named Hungan turns up on an unseaworthy tub called the 'Colendam' to steal the tin. The efforts to excavate the four *Iguanodons*, dinosaur carcasses perfectly preserved in oil by some prehistoric catastrophe, introduces a slight fantasy element into the book. The

Times Literary Supplement continued to be approving.[9] 'The troubles of navigating the unseaworthy "Colendam" are described vividly, it reads like a first hand description. Love-making abounds, and the book ends with a wedding (not Coulson's, he is evidently to be the hero of more books), but the author is content to regard women as unaccountable although delightful.'

However, Coulson was not to be the hero of any-further tales, for 'Jack Mann' would turn his talents on a new character who has secured him a firm place in the halls of remembrance for fantasy writers. The curious point is that while 'Jack Mann' was producing his Coulson series, the *Times Literary Supplement* enthusiastically (with one exception) reviewed them. But none of the eight books featuring his new hero went noticed by them.

The first book featuring the new character was certainly no taster for the seven more that were to come. It was more in the tradition of a Coulson thriller. Gregory George Gordon Green, known as 'Gees' from the four 'Gs' of his name, is a flippant young man with an odd sense of humour. He is the son of General Green, has seen some military service, is able to fly an aircraft, and has also served in the police force, achieving the rank of sergeant. This irritated his class-influenced military father who does not see the role of a policeman as a pursuit fit for gentlemen. The old general had disowned him when he refused to manage the family estate in Shropshire. But Gees has now left the police and sets up as a 'confidential agent' at 37 Little Oakfield Street, Haymarket, SW1. He has employed a pretty secretary—Eve Madeleine Brandon.

Gees' First Case, published by Wright and Brown in October 1936, starts off with Gees meeting the mysterious Christine Lenoir on a train. She comes to consult him but he finds an ex-colleague, Detective Inspector Tott, on his doorstep warning him off any interest in Miss Lenoir. Christine Lenoir is involved in a Masonic movement, which is pro Soviet, which plans a campaign to create revolution in Britain. They are going to bomb key industries, and specifically the Battersea and Lots Road Power Stations. It is a fascinating coincidence that three years later the IRA, in their fifteen-month bombing campaign, starting in 1939, did just this. Murder and mayhem follow. Gees brings in his friend Tony Briggs of the Foreign Office and winds up obtaining the arrest of the sinister Leonid Denghisovski and his partner Nikolai Smirilov. Christine Lenoir is allowed to flee to Switzerland while Gees helps himself to Denghisovski's funds of £10,000 to help finance his detective agency.

From this first novel, one is prepared for a Coulson type of hero engaged simply in action adventure or mystery thrillers. The second Gees adventure *Grey Shapes*, published in March 1937, came as a surprise to readers. Jack Mann plunges them into a weird fantasy with lycanthropy as the subject. Gees is consulted by Philip Tyrrell, a gentleman farmer of Cumberland. Wolf-like creatures are destroying his sheep, but there is more to it. Gees meets Tyrrell's strange neighbours, Diarmid and Gyda McCoul who live in a half-ruined castle, Locksborough. Gees eventually traps the wolves and they are killed. The dead forms assume the human shape of the McCouls. They are werewolves, seven hundred years old, having lived at the ruins of Locksborough since the reign of Henry III.

From then on the Gees stories took their weird fantasy format and won support of devotees of the genre. In *Nightmare Farm* (September 1937) Gees is consulted by Angus Hunter of Shropshire who relates that Denlandham, where he is a large landowner, is infested with ghostly phenomena. May Norris, a young woman, has been seized by a bodiless evil which controls her actions. The malevolent elements originate from the lost valley of Kir-Asa, the location of Vivian's novel *City of Wonder*. Gees arranges an exorcism. Knightsmere Farm, called Nightmare Farm by the locals, is the seat of the evil. Gees finds in it a secret room containing the preserved body of an ancestor of Angus Hunter. The corpse, freed from the malevolent force, disintegrates and Gees deposits its remains in a bottomless swamp.

The next Gees adventure, *The Kleinert Case*, published in February 1938, and republished in March 1939, has become so rare that not even the US publisher Joe Amadeo (d. 1980), reprinting all the Gees stories under his imprint Bookfinger between 1960–80, could find a copy to take a text from. This was the only Gees title not reprinted by Bookfinger. However, when Ramble House, in the USA, started to reprint the Jack Mann titles, they were able to reprint it in 2012. The story starts with an unprepossessing German character named Adolph Kleinert, who comes to consult Gees from Snoddlesdon, Kent. He wants someone to protect him but, at first, he is not specific as to what threatens him. He mentions that he needs the same sort of protection that Gees was able to give in 'Nightmare Farm'; so we have a hint of what is to come. He wants someone to prevent the theft of 'the great work of my life'. It is soon obvious however, dark forces are at work and the threat is far more than Gees bargains for.

In *Maker of Shadows* (November 1938) Gees is summoned to a remote Scottish hamlet by Miss Margaret Aylener and asked to free her niece of the spell of Gamel MacMorn. MacMorn lives at Brachmornalachan, surrounded by three monoliths and a Druidic circle, and Gees learns that the place is the site of a worship even older than Druidism. The character of Mac Morn is represented as an ageless survival from man's infancy on earth who has to sacrifice humans whose souls, or life essence, he must absorb to survive. The souls of his victims are released to become shadows which haunt the region. In the very moment of Margaret Aylener's niece's sacrifice, she is rescued by Gees, who brings an end to MacMorn and his immortality.

The Ninth Life (June 1939) is a first class supernatural fantasy worthy of Haggard and with a little touch of She about it. Tony Briggs is due to marry a mysterious woman called Cleo Kefra from Alexandria. Gees is intrigued when his father, General Sir George Green, lunching with Gees when Briggs and Cleo enter their restaurant, later declares that she is the very same girl who saved his life in Egypt some thirty years before.

As the story unfolds we find that Cleo was a priestess of Sekhmet, the female lion-headed god of Abydos. Kefra was lusted after by the King Menkau-Ra. To escape, she makes a pact with the goddess who saves her and gives her immortality, saying she will endure so long as the goddess endures. 'For these my gifts, nine times shall she render up herself to me, each time a renewal through which her beauty shall not fail, and until the nine times are accomplished, this my covenant shall endure... So long as the gods of Egypt are known of men and an altar is served in Egypt, so long shall the covenant endure.'[10] The story features strange deaths and mutilations by two large species of cat, a woman's body with the head of a lioness is seen. Gees finds himself in love with Cleo who is something of a split personality—one moment a frightened, innocent girl and the next a powerful harridan able to perform feats of magic. There is a final car chase after Cleo and her urbane and mystical servant, Saleh. Seen in the car is the lion-headed woman. The car crashes and only the bodies of Cleo and Saleh are discovered.

'Crampton got out again.

'"You're sure about that mask, Mr Tott?" he asked.

'"It'll be somewhere in front," Tott answered. "We would have seen if they'd thrown it out while we were chasing the saloon—at least, they were in sight a good part of the way. A mask like a lion's head—like a lioness's head, I mean. I saw it quite plainly while she had hold of that man Drake. Covering all her head and neck as far down as the collar of the fur coat. Look in front."

'They stripped the driving compartment of the saloon as Crampton had already stripped the back but with no more result. Tott, standing beside Gees, observed—"That's funny. They must have thrown it out."

'Gees said—"They didn't throw it out."

'"But it's not there, man!" Tott protested.

'"No," Gees agreed tonelessly, "it's not there."[11]

In *The Glass Too Many* (July 1940) Gees arrives at Nortonsweir-Ferring Hall at the request of Sydnor Reed. Reed is chairman of a company owning mining and transport concerns from Brazil to New Guinea. Recently a maid has developed a homicidal mania and had to be certified. Now Reed's hand has begun to twitch uncontrollably. He believes he is going mad, too. Gees finds that Reed's father has recently died and in the will his partner, Bernard Lawson, has been named heir if Sydnor Reed dies. Lawson, it appears, is the illegitimate son of old man Reed and is already a partner in the firm together with George Symonds. Bernard has a wife, Rosamund, and a half-sister, Claire, who provides a romance for Gees but then Claire is murdered. Rosamund is at the heart of it all, poisoning a variety of people with Lakiti and in the denouement Rosamund confessed to the killings and stabs herself with scissors impregnated with poison. The background is Gothic, with ancient tombs beneath the Hall. In this story, the fantasy is kept minimal with Gees being warned of danger by his secretary Eve Madeleine Brandon after she has had a premonition in a dream. But in the end it is a straightforward murder, for Rosamund has set out to kill Reed so that her husband, Bernard, will inherit.

The last Gees novel *Her Ways Are Death* was due for publication in the Spring of 1941. Typically, it has become the subject of a mystery concerning publication.

It is, thankfully, one Vivian mystery that we can now solve.

The story is one of Jack Mann's best. Gees is summoned by Jeremy St Pol Naylor of Troyarbour Hall, Blandford, Dorset, who claims Ira Warren is a witch and 'her ways are death'. Naylor himself claims to be a Volsung, a descendant of Oger the Nailer, a half-god half-mortal, a son of Odin by a mortal woman. Ira is a descendant of Wulfrunna, Oger's wife, and descended from a line of witches who have killed Naylor's ancestors. Ira is now after him.

Gees, of course, falls for Ira who is, indeed, a witch, and has a cherry coloured cat named Peter. Love makes Gees immune to her powers and wakes another being in herself. She has to choose between the occult powers and Gees. The age-old feud between Ira and Naylor draws to a close when Naylor steals the Rod of An from the lost city of Atlantis and in doing so is struck down by a monstrous figure of the god Thor. Ira continues to worship the occult powers, promising to return to Gees when she is able. There is a frightening apparition in Gees' office and he finds strands of her black hair after the vision has departed. Hell has claimed its own. Disbelieving, however, Gees hurries to her cottage Dorset and finds it desolate. Only Peter the cat remains and Gees returns to London with it.

In the course of this novel one cannot help feeling sorry for Eve Madeleine Brandon, Gees' secretary, who is clearly in love with him.

The mystery of *Her Ways Are Death*, is that there is no catalogue evidence for its existence. The first edition would have been a 7s.6d volume. Only a 4s.6d. volume in reprint jacket has been discovered with a first edition Spring 1941 catalogue bound inside the book, which announces the 7s.6d publication. What had happened was that the offices of Wright and Brown, at 4 Farringdon Avenue, had been bombed and all their records and much of their stock had been destroyed by fire. The raid had happened on the night of December 29/30 1940, two days after Vivian's main publishers Ward Lock had been hit by two explosive bombs and their warehouse reduced to ashes, which we will examine further in chapter eleven.

Messrs Wright and Brown, however, were able to move to smaller premises at 1 Crane Court, Fleet Street. They carried on their business until the 1960s when the firm simply folded and vanished. Copies of *Her Ways Are Death* survived the bombing. Doubtless, the 7s.6d jackets had been destroyed. It was therefore decided to issue the surviving copies some months later in first edition binding, but with a 4s.6d reprint jacket. The book, therefore, appeared unnoticed by either the *English Catalogue* or the USA *Catalogue of Books in Print*, nor even was there a copy deposited in the British Library.

It was a sad note on which to end the run of 'Jack Mann' novels.

It was 'Jack Mann' who has gathered a devoted following in the USA. Otis Adelbert Kline (1891–1946), a prolific adventure writer for the American 'pulps' had set up a successful literary agency, Otis Kline Associates. He represented the work of H.G. Wells and many other noted authors. Much of his own fiction was in the realms of fantastic adventures such as his most successful novel *The Call of the Jungle*, made into a film with Dorothy Lamour, in which she first appeared in her famous sarong, and which translated to a radio serial. Kline was enthused by the early 'Jack Mann' novels and took on the representation of 'Jack Mann' in the USA. It seems his first successes, however, were placing two of Vivian's 'Inspector Head' thrillers, which we will discuss in the following chapter. A chance copy of *Grey*

Shadows, marked as a file copy of Kline's Fifth Avenue agency, now in the hands of Jack Adrian, brought for the confirmation of Kline's involvement with Vivian from Kitty Vivian.[12]

In 1939, he sold both the *Ninth Life* and *Maker of Shadows* to the prestigious *Argosy* magazine as serials. *The Ninth Life* ran from August 5–26 while *Maker of Shadows* ran from December 9 1939 to January 6 1940. At the same time he was able to sell '*Count Caspar*', which Vivian had written for *Adventure-Story* as 'Galbraith Nicholson' to *Golden Fleece* in May 1939, which then appeared as by E. Charles Vivian. This period was a good one for both Vivian and 'Jack Mann' in the US market.

When Oscar Friend took over the agency after Kline's death, he was able to sell Vivian's *City of Wonder* to *Famous Fantastic Mysteries* (October 1947), and *Fields of Sleep* (appearing in August 1949), as *The Valley of Silent Men*, and *Her Ways are Death* (June 1952). He later resold *The Ninth Life* to *A. Merritt's Fantasy Magazine* (April 1950).

While Godwin had published in book form one Jack Mann novel, *The Dead Man's Chest*s, in 1934, and Ryerson's of Toronto had issued a spurious American edition of *Detective Coulson* in 1936 (this was just an imported number of the UK edition), it was not until 1970 that the New York firm of Bookfinger began to reprint the whole of the Gees' series, with the one exception of the scarce volume, *The Kleinert Case*.

'Jack Mann' books became highly prized collectors' items with recent first editions, in the early 1990s, selling in the region of £250 in the USA and with comparative prices from UK dealers.

There seems no reason why Vivian should cease writing 'Jack Mann' novels after 1941. Wright and Brown had been bombed but they were still continuing their business from new premises. And the Jack Mann' novels were certainly selling, although it seems that the Coulson titles had gone to more editions per title than the 'Gees' mysteries.

According to Kitty Vivian: 'I do not know why he gave up the Jack Mann books, but probably because he felt he had come to the end of that line and wanted to do something different.'[13] The career of 'Jack Mann' had spanned eight years and produced fourteen titles, seven of which no historiographer of weird fiction can afford to ignore.

Notes

1. *Armchair Detective*, 1972, p. 21.
2. *Ibid.*
3. *Times Literary Supplement*, March 2, 1933.
4. *Times Literary Supplement*, October 12, 1933.
5. *English Catalogue of Books*, London, Vol. xiv, ed. James D. Stewart.
6. *Times Literary Supplement*, March 15, 1934.
7. *Times Literary Supplement*, July 18, 1935.
8. *Ibid.*
9. *Times Literary Supplement*, May 30, 1036.
10. *The Ninth Life*, Jack Mann, Wright & Brown, London, 1939, p. 109.
11. *Ibid.* p. 281/282.
12. Katharine Vivian Ashton, to author, April 14, 1994.
13. Katharine Vivian Ashton, letter to author, November 23, 1993.

CHAPTER TEN

INSPECTOR HEAD OF WESTINGBOROUGH

If we discount the creations of 'Jack Mann', for no critic or member of the reading public knew at the time that this was a pseudonym of Vivian, one fictional character created Vivian's reputation as a first class writer of detective mysteries during the 1930s. It was the creation of Inspector Jeremy Head of Westingborough. The Head stories, a dozen novels published between 1934 and 1939, are excellent, well-crafted mysteries that were deserving of the critical recognition they received from critics as diverse as Dorothy L. Sayers to Will Cuppy. Had Vivian concentrated primarily on producing Head tales then he might have won more lasting fame than fell to his lot. The books were not just good genre fare but in such titles as *Seventeen Cards* they rise to such excellence that they can be favourably compared with products of many mystery writers of his era whose titles are still popularly reprinted today.

Head could certainly hold his own with Inspector Roderic Alleyn created by Ngaio Marsh (1899–1982). He is not a propagandist as G.K. Chesterton (1874–1936), whose 'Father Brown' is still popular. Vivian, in truth, is a better storyteller than Agatha Christie (1890–1976), and a more deft plotter than Margery Allingham (1904–1966). One wonders how much John Creasey's (1908–1973) 'Inspector West' owed, consciously or unconsciously, to 'Inspector Head'. But if they were so good, why then have the Head novels disappeared from our ken?

Head was a fully rounded character. He is described as an alert looking, tall, middle-aged man, always dressed well, and usually in blue-serge. He is married to a lady called Emily but, while his wife is referred to, she never makes an appearance. It is a device that the writer of the Lieutenant Colombo American detective series, broadcast on television from 1971, used with equally good effect. Interestingly, however, in the last novel *Touch and Go*, Emily has disappeared and Inspector Head, who states he is forty-six years old, heads off into the sunset with Avril Madison, aged twenty-nine years old.

'Wadden stood quite still to watch them go. He saw Avril's hand on Head's shoulder as she looked up and his head leant toward her.

'"Gosh!" he murmured. "My old lady'll throw a fit and then start singin' anthems. Loverly eyes—but she's the luckier of the two."'

Avril is the adopted daughter of wealthy factory owner, Henry Madison, who is strangled as the story opens. Head solves the case and Avril offers him the job as manager of the late Madison's factory to fund Head's desire to study and write a book on the psychology of crime. It's a strange ending to the 12 book career of the country police inspector.

We are told that Head is actually a cousin by marriage of Vivian's other detective creation, Inspector Terence Herbert Byrne of Scotland Yard. The relationship is clearly spelt out in the first novel where Byrne's Aunt Gertie is the mother of Head's wife Emily. Head's territory is the small industrial town of Westingborough, which we can place on the Hertfordshire and Bedfordshire border. We are told that Head 'knew all the country round about Westingborough for miles, as a fox knows his coverts or a lion his hunting grounds.'[1] Westingborough, lying in the Idleburn valley, the next railway stop on the line from Crandon, is equally as important as the human characters in these novels. We get to know Westingborough, its railway station and staff, its hostelries, such as 'The Duke of York' opposite the police station run by Mrs Nell Cummin, known as 'Little Nell'. We know also the outlying areas; the village of Carden, for example, which does not boast a police station but comes under Westingborough's jurisdiction. We get to know almost every yard of the road as it climbs across Condor Hill, passing the big house called Condor Grange.

In the *Rainbow Puzzle* (1938) Vivian describes the town thus:

'Certain special properties in the waters of the little River Idleburn were responsible, originally, for raising Westingborough from the status of a small agricultural centre to its present position as a thriving town of some fourteen thousand inhabitants. It was discovered that these waters facilitated and improved the dyeing of fine fabrics, and thus Nevile-dyed products became famous, and the town become mainly industrial in character and grew to its present dimensions. Closely analogous, on a large scale, is the reputation of West of England serges and Burton beers and ales; modern research and syntheses have gone far beyond these initial discoveries, but the industries, firmly established, persist. In the case of Westingborough, the town extends its tentacles into the surrounding country, and goes on growing, taking more and more of the rising ground on each side of the river valley, which, however, outside the radius of industrial influences, is still agricultural and pastoral in character.

'To the west boundary on that side of the Idleburn drainage basin, the long ridge of Condor Hill is the highest point runs roughly north and south, and, cut off from the earliest rays of the morning sun by the mass of the hill, Carden village nestles under its western slope, south west from Westingborough and some eight or nine miles distant from the town. In earlier times, the main London Road followed the river valley so as to miss Carden, but a new road, cut over the northern shoulder of Condor Hill, now descends in such a way that the widened village street is taken in, and the old coach road father southward is no more than a little used, tree shaded lane. The new road winds up and down the height, its gradient eased by a sixty foot cutting at the summit; on the Carden side, enough of a small plateau has been taken in, macadamized, and railed at its edge to form a parking place beside the road; every summer weekend, the number of visitors parking there to survey the beauty of the valley in which Carden is set is such as to attract at least a couple of ice-cream barrows and a perambulating mineral-water-and-bun trader both for

Saturday afternoon and Sunday, and, during the week, some half dozen or more cars and motor cycle combinations may be found halted there at any reasonable hour.'[2]

So vivid are Vivian's portrayals of the Westingborough area that they remind one of a place one has known, a place whose name is on the tip of one's tongue and yet... On page 39 of *Accessory After* Vivian even has a sketch map of the location. To stop such speculation Vivian took the unusual step of writing an author's note in *Who Killed Gatton?* (1936), to state 'All characters and localities in this story are entirely imaginary'. His characters often reappear in their various roles; the person who runs the local inn, the local architect, estate agent, shopkeepers and others. One had a feeling of a small stable country community as they used to exist prior to the Second World War.

In charge of the police station in Westingborough is Head's boss, Superintendent Henry 'Bulgy' Wadden, 'sixteen stone of solidity', 'with a roll of flesh bulging over the top edge of his uniform collar' but with 'keen, apparently fierce eyes'. Wadden is approaching retirement and his dream is to buy some land with his wife and start a market garden specialising in tomatoes grown under glass. He seems always about to make a decision about the day of retirement but draws back each time. He is a somewhat self-indulgent character, which is sometimes mistaken for laziness. He often gets resentful of the number of murders Westinborough has to deal with.

The first Head novel was published by Ward Lock in January 1934. *Shadow on the House* was not so much a 'whodunnit' as a 'howdunnit'. It is clear from an early point that Hector Forrest, managing director of Nevile and Forest, has attempted to kill his partner Raymond Nevile but, by chance, Nevile's secretary, Phyllis Harland, has become the victim instead of her employer. The device is ingenious, an explosive is triggered when she lifts a telephone receiver. Head suspects Forrest but cannot bring a case against him. Then a tramp finds a small, green clock in a stream. Head then tracks a series of clues, which constitute his case. Against this, we have Dorothy Morland of Long Ridge, Westingborough Parva—and

Nevile provides a romance against the mystery. The *Times Literary Supplement* approved of it. 'The detective methods are well described, logical and convincing.'[3]

Vivian's choice of a dedication for the book is interesting. Sir Henry Royce (1863–1933), the partner of C.S. Rolls, had just died. Vivian dedicated *Shadow on the House* to his memory with the epithet 'Genius, Whose Works Endure'. We can only speculate that Vivian, in his days as editor of *Flying*, must have met Royce at that time when he had turned the attention of the Rolls-Royce firm to aero-engines. This acquaintanceship brings into question the authenticity of 'Harrison Royce' writing in Vivian's *Mystery-Story* in January 1924, with a story '*Sand in Egypt*'. I think we are safe to say that this was another Vivian pseudonym.

Accessory After was the second Head novel published in September 1934. Vivian dedicated it to his agent—'to my friend John Farquharson'.

When Edward Ensor Carter, the new owner of the Grange, is found shot in the early hours of the morning, Head is called in. The evening before he has given a small party, all of whom have a dislike of the man, and his four domestic servants and the chauffeur are not over-fond of him. As Head investigates, and his cousin Inspector Byrne is brought into the case, he finds Carter was Eddie Ensor, a theatrical agent and producer who was certainly not a nice person. Vengeance is the theme and the suspects are numerous but, of course, Head eventually finds the least likely person who has pulled the trigger.

It is with his third Head novel that Vivian established the excellence of the series. Yet in this work, *Seventeen Cards* (January 1935), Head does not even appear on the scene until Chapter 16 (on page 262). Vivian, with tremendous skill, has already sketched out all we need to know of the suspects for the murder, given us all the clues and red-herrings, and allows Head to arrive as the catalyst who produces the murderer within the very last sentences of the book. It is a first rate, 'cracking' mystery and one of his most atmospheric and tautly written tales.

The story starts with Montagu Kemp, a lawyer, and Diane Heriot, an actress and singer, arriving late one winter evening at Crandon railway station. They do not know each other but both are invited as weekend guests at the mansion of Castel Garde, owned by Houghton, a successful businessman of shady reputation. A blizzard is blowing and snowdrifts add to the dangers. They introduce themselves and join forces to persuade a local taxi driver named 'Mad Andy' to drive them along the rural lanes to the isolated house. The terrors of the night drive through drifting snow is a gripping piece of narration.

There are seventeen guests at Castel Garde, now completely cut off from civilisation. The guests are nearly all the financial victims, discarded mistresses, or enemies in one way or another of a man who is attempting to blackmail the host and his current mistress. The guests are called upon to while away the evening, after dinner, by a murder game. Cards are dealt to the players. The person who draws the knave of spades is to be the murderer and the drawer of the king of diamonds will represent the detective. After the cards are drawn, the lights are extinguished. The murderer must touch his victim who will scream. The lights then go up and the detective has to trace the assassin. Everyone must tell the truth except the murderer. The game therefore proceeds. The lights are extinguished, there is a cry. But when the lights go on again, one of the guests (no prizes for guessing who) has truly been murdered—'a shining, black hafted antique dagger had been driven through his shirt front and deep into his breast'.

Among the critics to acclaim this novel was Dorothy L. Sayers. (1893–1957), the creator of the urbane, aristocratic sleuth, Lord Peter Wimsey. She was not only a detective storywriter, but an essayist on medieval and Christian subjects and the translator of Dante's *Divine Comedy*. She was among the first women to be awarded an Oxford degree. Writing in the *Sunday Times* she said of *Seventeen Cards*:

'The vigour of the narrative and the fine sense of strain and tension produced by the interplay of nearly twenty characters, who all suspect one another, make the telling anything but commonplace.

'The thrills all spring from the one central situation—there is no reckless adding of blood to blood—and the action is confined to the one place and to a few breathless hours. When the pent-up emotions of the suspects are about to break out into hysteria, our old friend Inspector Head arrives and solves the mystery.'

Torquemada, the heroic name hid the identity of a well-respected *Observer* critic, wrote: 'No grateful reader—and we all at one time or another have felt grateful to Mr Vivian—can at all find fault with his latest favourite, Inspector Head, or with the continued and frequently published ingenuities of Inspector Head's creator.'[7]

In January 1936, Ward Lock produced *Who Killed Gratton*. Superintendent Wadden discovers an apparently abandoned aircraft near Condor Grange. But the body of the pilot, identified as Harry Gratton, is lying dead nearby. The aircraft is the 'Zalescz Stratosphere', which embodies so many revolutionary secrets that the builders of the machine assure Wadden that Gatton was undoubtedly murdered by foreign agents. But why has Gatton landed in this deserted area when under strict orders not to land outside of his own aerodrome in the experimental machine? Inspector Head finds the reason in the person of Miss Sheila Bell and comes to the solution through a maze of a strange drama of human emotions. 'Two particular achievements distinguish this book', observed the *Times Literary Supplement*, 'it suggests a really ingenious and plausible "revolutionary aircraft", and it presents—perhaps unintentionally—a further strong argument for the reform of procedure in coroners' courts.'[8]

Other critics were, a little more fulsome. The *Evening News* felt it 'A good sound exciting story, with enough trouble taken over the characters to make them play their parts vividly.'[9] *Truth* recommended it 'as a murder-mystery thriller, well above the average, may be commended to all who are addicted to this class of fiction. The reader's interest and curiosity being well held throughout.'[10] The Sunday *Referee* made the general comment that 'Mr Charles Vivian's Inspector Head books are rapidly rising in critical esteem among all readers who love a good story with plenty of thrills and a water tight plot.'[11]

Vivian dedicated the book to F.S. Rainer 'whose friendship, through many years, has not failed'. The Rainer in question does not seem to be related to the Louis Rainer who married Enid Clarke, his niece. Vivian had in fact made a hand written dedication in one of his books 'to my friend F.S. Rainer' as early as September 5 1925.[12] Kitty Vivian is unable to identify her father's friend.

The next Head novel *With Intent to Kill* (July 1936) is a curiosity because it is rewritten from an earlier book. In 1934, Vivian had sold a novella entitled *House for Sale* to Amalgamated Press' *Thriller* Library. It was a 94 pager with eighteen chapters.

The curiosity is that only two years after the publication of this novella, Vivian has added four more chapters to reach the standard Ward Lock format and sold it to them as *With Intent to Kill*. How had he managed a rights reversion in such short a space of time?

Once more, Head is in good form. Mr Guddle of Guddle and Cheek, house agents and surveyors, is showing a prospective buyer over an empty country house just outside Garden village on the Crandon Road. They notice an unpleasant smell and in one of the rooms they come across the body of a dead man with his skull smashed in. He has obviously been murdered. The opening chapter is remarkably like the opening sequence in Val Guest's murder mystery movie 'Jigsaw' (1962), starring Jack Warner.

It is the holiday season but Wadden and Head have another murder on their hands. Vivian's humour shows through here when he makes Wadden exclaim: '"Head, we're getting more than our fair share. This is the fourth murder in this district inside two years, and two of 'em are strangers who came here to be killed. Y'know, we ought to get a poster out."

'"A poster?" Head inquired dubiously.

'"Fine hunting district, beautiful scenery, healthy air—come to the Westingborough district and get murdered. Every facility offered."'[13]

The first step is to identify the corpse, a stranger to the area, and then follow the clues and discount the red-herrings until Head reveals the murderer. But then things are not entirely proved until a court case denouement in which Vivian has Sir Herbert Eustace lead for the defence. Eustace is a character which Vivian was to bring back in his last thriller *Vain Escape* (1952). The *Times Literary Supplement* pointed out: 'In some detective novels everything is a clue, but Mr Vivian does not limit himself so closely.'[14]

Tramp's Evidence was published in January 1937. This became the first Head novel sold by Otis Kline to the US where it was re-titled *Barking Dog Mystery*, published by Hillman Curl of New York in their Clue Club Mystery series. The main figure in the book is a tramp named Mister Napoleon Marvel. The tramp is rather like Mister Thomas Marvel who appears in chapter nine of H. G. Well's classic *The Invisible Man* (1897).

Vivian was obviously a fan of Herbert George Wells (1866–1946) and was now sharing Wells' US agent, Otis Adelbert Kline. Perhaps he even knew Wells. Vivian's daughter confirms: 'My father often spoke of H. G. Wells and they probably did meet—I know he liked Wells' work.' Vivian's classic weird short story '*Ancient Evil*', published in *Mystery-Story Magazine*, November 1923, had, as its protagonist, 'Hubert' Wells. The same character 'Hubert' Wells appeared in '*A Swamp Survival*', in *Colour*, January 1925.

Vivian's Mr Napoleon Marvel, like the Wells' character, disliked work or washing but liked other people's chickens. But he is quite incapable of murder or torture. Yet young PC Vale has found him in The Grey House, the secluded home of Bernard Wymering, with his knife all bloody and Wymering's still warm corpse at his feet. Inspector Head knows better than to accept Marvel's guilt and sets out to track down the real culprit. But is it Allday, whose wife is having an affair with Wymering, or a band of fanatic Moslems whose faith Wymering has outraged?[15]

The next Head novel was *.38 Automatic* published in August 1937. Vivian likes his dark and stormy nights and he describes them well. On such a night a local taxi-driver parks his cab outside Westinborough police station just as Superintendent Wadden and Inspector Head are crossing the road to the station. Tanner, the driver, informs them that someone had shot his fare. The man is dead. He had picked the man up at the railway station and was told to drive to Westingborough Parva. The storm had muffled the sound of the shot. A tree blocked the road and the driver found the corpse and returned to the police station. The dead man is a local, Frederick Dickson, married and respectable. Head has a difficult case on his hands but doggedly pursues a tangled skein of love triangles, bigamy and vengeance, until he comes on the most unlikely suspect who is revealed as the killer.

Evidence in Blue (January 1938) was also sold to the US to Hillmann Curl, re-titled *Man in Gray* and produced for the Clue Club Mystery series. Later that year it was also published as a 90 cent paperback by MacLeod's. In previous books we have met 'Little Nell' Cummins who came as a barmaid to the Duke of York Hotel, the principal hotel in Westingborough when Old Bragg was proprietor. He left the hotel to her in his will. The story starts with her crossing the road to the police station opposite to inform Superintendent Wadden that a man has been found stabbed to death in Room No 7. Head is sent to investigate.

The man is identified as Feilding [sic] of Arnold Haussbrant, a firm of importers. The story develops, with blackmail and sisterly sacrifice, through a really exciting pace to a surprise ending in which all our sympathies are finally with the killer. While ignored by leading critics in England, the American edition received a warm welcome. 'A great deal of assiduous clue-chasing and competent writing,' observed the US *Review of Literature*.[16] 'The story is skilfully planned and well told, the suspense being sustained up to the final chapter, all without any undue use of red herrings,' commended Isaac Anderson in the *New York Times*, who chose it as his lead recommendation in his column '*New Mystery Stories*'.[17] The famous critic and humorist Will Cuppy noticed it in *The New York Herald Tribune Books* but felt it was only a 'middling item',[18] *The New Yorker*[19] commented that it was a 'pleasant' and 'reliable story of murder' with Head as 'the conscientious sleuth'.

Evidence in Blue remains one of the best Head tales in which the detective is allowed full range of his deductive abilities.

The Rainbow Puzzle was published in September 1938. While the *Times Literary Supplement* did not think it was well written and 'the actual criminal device involved is not very novel, and the extreme reluctance of the police to investigate is overdone—it is a sound and not impossible story.[20]

Jim Chalfont and Tony Wilson live at The Firs at Todlington near Westingborough. They are inventors and have perfected a screen which creates a natural colour for movie film. They are in the hands of an unscrupulous financier, George Newton Logan, who has a contract with them, which will deprive them of the rewards of their ingenuity. Soon after he visits them, he disappears and his daughter believes he is dead. In fact, the story is well-written and the local descriptions are excellent. There is a good scene in 'The Four Feathers', the local pub at Todlington, which starts:

'Thus, in the first of the dusk, he reached "The Four Feathers", a gaunt looking, two storied erection of dingy red brick with uncurtained windows, set back from the road, and shaded by a couple of tall fir trees. Thorn swerved his car off the road towards the entrance of the inn, and instantly found himself in dry, loose sand that slowed him to a walking pace, while the back wheels skidded, gripped, skidded again, and then took him on with a rush that nearly crashed him against the open doorway. Averting that mishap, he switched off his engine, got out, and entered the place. The room on the right of the doorway, he found by looking in, was untenanted; he opened the door on the left, and found himself in an atmosphere heavy with shag tobacco smoke. A counter ran across the inner end of the room, and behind it stood a heavy-jowled man in his shirt sleeves; two youngsters were playing darts at the end by the window, and between them and the counter four men sat at little tables, each with a mug of beer before him, while two more leaned against the counter with yet more mugs. It seemed to Thorn that a hint of conversation suspended by his entry hung in the smoke-laden air, and that all regarded him with bucolic resentment, as a stranger intruding on what was almost a family gathering.'[21]

Head's investigation brings a surprise conclusion. As Dr Bennett remarks:

'"A most unsatisfactory case for you, Head."

'"You forget—such an end as this saves all the expense of a trial,"' is Head's cynical response. The *Times Literary Supplement* critic notwithstanding, *The Rainbow Puzzle* is an excellent tale.

January 1939, saw the publication of the eleventh Inspector Head novel in *Problem By Rail*. The problem is that a man is found murdered and mutilated in an express train while a naked man is found in the next carriage suffering from the effect of a drug. Head investigates and discovers that the murderer has stripped the murdered man of his own clothes and dressed the body in the clothes of the now naked one. Why the murderer should take this trouble and the pull the communication cord before disappearing is obscure. Head encounters problems and there is even talk that Scotland Yard should be brought it.

'One great virtue of Mr Vivian's stories,' said the *Times Literary Supplement* 'is the character of the somewhat lazy Superintendent at Westingborough whose extreme resentment whenever a murder is committed in his area is well depicted.'[22] *Problem by Rail*, which has another cameo appearance by Head's cousin, Inspector Byrne, is yet a further enjoyable addition to the Head *ouvrage*.

The last Head story was published in the month that Britain declared war on Hitler's Germany, September 1939. This was *Touch and Go* in which Head not only gets his man but ends by going off with the heroine Avril Madison while Superintendent Wadden obtains his heart's desire, a new home to retire to, to grow tomatoes—under glass. But before that Head has a difficult case to solve with the murder of Henry Madison. It was a good ending to the series but why did Vivian decide to finished what was, in many people's estimation, his best creation and one he should still be more widely remembered for? Again, we find another mystery. Inspector Head was eliminated while his cousin Inspector Byrne continued to play shadowy roles in subsequent books.

Notes

1. *Who Killed Gatton*, 1936, p. 10.
2. *The Rainbow Puzzle*, 1939, p. 122/123.
3. *Times Literary Supplement.* February 15, 1934.
4. *Sunday Times.* January 13, 1935.
5. *Daily Telegraph*, January 30, 1935.
6. *Public Opinion*, February 1935.
7. *Observer*, October 6, 1935.
8. *Times Literary Supplement.* February 15, 1936.
9. *Evening News*, January 29, 1936.
10. *Truth*, February 7, 1936.
11. *The Sunday Referee*, January 26, 1936.
12. *A Spectrum of Fantasy*, George Locke, Ferret Fantasy, London, 1980. p. 219.
13. *With Intent to Kill*, p. 29.
14. *Times Literary Supplement*, August 29, 1936.
15. *Times Literary Supplement*, January 23, 1927.
16. *Review of Literature*, June 25, 1938.
17. *The New York Times*, June 19, 1938.
18. *New York Herald Tribune Books*, New York, June 19, 1938.
19. *New Yorker*, July 2, 1938.
20. *Times Literary Supplement*, September 17, 1938.
21. *The Rainbow Puzzle*, p. 155/156.
22. *Times Literary Supplement*, June 14, 1939.

CHAPTER ELEVEN

THE LAST YEARS

The last fourteen years of Vivian's life, following the result of the blackmail case in 1933, were spent industriously. According to Kitty Vivian, it was a quiet period. Vivian did not travel much. He still enjoyed tinkering with his car, a Morris saloon in which he taught Kitty to drive, and taking Marion to visit Eden Phillpotts in his Devonshire home and other friends whose names Kitty Vivian cannot recall. One person that Vivian and his wife did call on in neighbouring Somerset was Archibald Thomas Pechey (1876–1961), better known as both 'Valentine' and 'Mark Cross'. Pechey lived at Ivy House, West Shepton, Shepton Mallet. When he died on November 29, 1961, his output had been prolific not only as 'Valentine', taken from his mother's name of Vallentin, but as 'Mark Cross' for under this name he had published 47 detective thrillers for Ward Lock. His obituary was carried by *The Times*, November 30, 1961. Vivian and Pechey shared John Farquharson as their literary agent.

Speaking of her father, Kitty Vivian says: 'Apart from a small circle of friends, he had only a limited though faithful readership.'[1] Another member of that small circle of friends was the family doctor, John F. Sharpe MB, to whom Vivian dedicated *Man With A Scar* because Sharpe had 'provided the idea out of which this book grew'.

The Vivians did little entertaining at their home, apart from the occasional drinks party. Vivian liked dining out and one favourite restaurant was The Pheasantry Club in Chelsea. The Pheasantry

Club, housed in a Georgian building in King's Road, was regarded as a meeting place for people in the arts and literary world. Dylan Thomas, Augustus John and other prominent figures were frequent patrons. A lot of evenings were spent at the house of a close friend, Louis J. MacQuilland, in Chelsea. Kitty Vivian recalls 'he was very hard up—he was, I think, a writer or journalist'. Indeed, Louis MacQuilland (1873–1951) had been a leading critic and a poet originally from Belfast. He was best known for his volume *A Song of the Open Road* (London, 1916) but had not published anything in volume form since then. He was well respected, appearing in the *Literary Yearbook* and *Who's Who in Literature* from 1906 until 1934. Apparently, Vivian enjoyed his company very much. MacQuilland died at his Chelsea home in 1951.

Another means of relaxation was carpentry and joinery with Vivian making several small pieces of furniture, such as tables, which are still kept in his family. When he was working he had no strict routine but worked all hours and days when he was engaged in a book. He would sometimes show his work to his wife and daughter as he wrote it, chapter by chapter.

Vivian was a heavy smoker and drank a lot of tea while working, but not coffee. Kitty Vivian's view of him was as a sweet-natured person, entirely without malice, generous but who could be roused to anger at injustice. She felt that he had a naturally artistic temperament. He was an avid reader, especially of contemporary writers, but, particularly he enjoyed the works of Rudyard Kipling, G. K. Chesterton and H. G. Wells, presumably forgiving the latter's Socialism.

But being away at boarding school and then going to live in France for a while, Kitty Vivian had little knowledge of the details of her father's life and work.

Many facts discovered by research have come as a surprise to her and, at times, she was inclined to deny them. She had never heard of her father's contentious novel *Passion Fruit*[2]. 'I have never heard of the Heinemann episode, nor of Heinemann publishing anything of his. It sounds highly improbable as though another author were concerned.'[3] 'I do not think that Sydney Barrie Lynd can be anything to do with my father.'[4] 'Galbraith Nicholson...Not only did I never hear this name mentioned by my father or anyone else; it has a thoroughly spurious sound to it, because Galbraith is a well-known family name, and in those days surnames were not commonly confused with first Christian names. It is highly unlikely that my father would have used such a pseudonym.'[5] Yet as early as May 1939, Vivian had been clearly identified as having used the 'Galbraith Nicholson' pseudonym.[6] Similarly, she steadfastly refused to believe that he also wrote the Barry Lynd western novels.

As pointed out, ten years ago many of those who attempted a Vivian bibliography did not realise that there were two writers named Charles Vivian working in the field of popular magazines. They were convinced all verses in the magazines were the work of E. Charles Vivian. I myself was initially persuaded until my friend and colleague Mike Ashley examined the evidence. When I originally put the question of the verses to ECV's daughter some twenty years ago, she was adamant that he did not write verse. As she had been so reticence in other areas, I am afraid that I failed to accept her statement. 'I am interested and surprised by what you tell me of my father's poetry. He never spoke of it, as I believe he would have, in response to my own interests and because we shared tastes in poetry, and I never heard of any either published or not. Are you sure the poems you have found are his work and not someone else's?'[7] She was, of course, correct.

In another letter[8] Kitty Vivian repeats that she knew nothing about his poetry, 'although he did discuss his other work, publishers and so forth with my mother and myself.

'When I was in my teens I was often away from home and out of touch with my parents.'

When seeking an explanation for the lack of personal publicity surrounding her father, Kitty Vivian commented: 'As for publicity, I really don't know why he did not have more—that may be something over which Ward Lock treated him badly. On the other hand, from the writing that I have done, I would guess that he may have found the process of getting publicity simply a great bore. He enjoyed writing, took a great interest in it, but all the business of marketing was up to publishers and agents.'

That being so, Kitty Vivian says: 'My father and I had big talks about books and writing. He wrote excellent English and gave me advice which I have remembered and put into practice to this day. He would discuss his current piece of work with my mother and myself. Although he was fond of poetry, he never mentioned writing any and I know nothing about this.'[9]

It does seem curious that Vivian never discussed with his daughter the facts of his childhood and relationship with his parents in spite of spending much of his writing clearly trying to come to terms with it in a fictionalised form. Kitty Vivian was 29 years old when her father died and, therefore, it was not that she was too young to discuss such matters. She had no idea that her father was staying with his own father when he died in 1930. She was then 13 years old, old enough to know that her grandfather had just died. Initially, Kitty Vivian had thought 'he broke off relations with his family early in my childhood'[10] and that 'he did not keep in touch with his sisters.'[11] Later she amended this and recalled that 'my father *did* keep in touch with his sisters, but apart from one or two occasions, they did not come to see us and relations with them were rather cool.'[12] Then 'Diana (Elizabeth Rosamond) I met only once or twice and we did not have much contact with her.'[13] If Elizabeth Rosamond had read *Ash* and recognised herself as 'Beth' and her husband Ashford Clarke as 'Arthur Ashford', one would think that there was reason enough for a coolness of relationships. Certainly something was wrong, for in the last years of Elizabeth Rosamond's life she was living but a walk from Vivian's flat in Longridge Road. Yet Vivian's daughter has no recollection of any regular visits and certainly Vivian did not take his family to visit this curious aunt whom Kitty Vivian only knew under the name 'Diana'. Even Olive, then living at 3 Gloucester Road, Teddington, was no more than a bus-ride away from Vivian's home.

It would appear, from Kitty Vivian's evidence, that after the death of Vivian's parents in 1929 and 1930, he and his sisters did drift apart, in spite of the closeness of their homes. Elizabeth Rosamond and her husband were living at 23 York Mansions, Battersea Park, SW11 until 1940. On April 1, 1939, Ashford Clarke, died of a haemorrhage of a duodenal ulcer, aged only 54 years. He had been rushed into the Royal Masonic Hospital, Hammersmith. His son 'Alan' Charles Clarke registered the death. Ashford left a sum of £2,519 in equal shares to his wife, his son 'Alan' Charles' and daughter Enid.[14]

Elizabeth Rosamond and Enid now moved into 4 Albert Palace Mansions, Lurline Gardens, near Battersea Park, SW11.

On February 25 1941, Elizabeth Rosamond's daughter, Enid Rosamund Lois 'Vincent-Clarke', then working as an ambulance driver and in the Air Raid Precautions, married 2nd Lt. Louis Thomas Rainer, of the Special Air Services Battalion, a mining engineer. He gave an address in Woodvale Road, Knutsford, and gave his father's name as Henry Louis Scott Rainer, a farmer. It seems likely that Lt. Rainer was a colonial, perhaps from South Africa. From Olive's will we can tell that they had a son, Alan Richard Rainer. But Enid married again to Ernest Harvey. Olive left £100 to go to the education of Enid's son Alan Rainer, which indicates that the boy had been born after the war. No birth certificate is extant in the UK, nor any death or divorce documentation on Louis Rainer. Nor, indeed, is there a marriage certificate for Enid and Ernest Harvey. Indeed, there is no sign of a birth certificate for Louis Rainer in this country. This would indicate that Louis came from another country and that Enid and Louis went abroad after the war and their child was born there.

Elizabeth Rosamond moved to the Hotel Stuart, Richmond, after her daughter's marriage. Perhaps it was to be nearer her sister, Olive, then living in Teddington. It was early in 1942 that the old complaint of tuberculosis, which Vivian made the cause of 'Beth's' death in *Ash*, triggered complications. On March 28 1942, Elizabeth Rosamund (under the name Rosamund Elizabeth Eliza Vincent-Clarke) died of lobar pneumonia and bronchiectasis induced by tuberculosis—the death certificate specifying the TB as an 'old' complaint. It was Olive, her sister, who registered the death.

These events went unknown to Kitty Vivian, who in 1990 was not aware whether her two aunts were still alive. Olive had not died until 1960, and it was her nephew 'Alan' Clarke who registered the death. 'Alan' was then living at 36 Manor Way, Chesham, Buckinghamshire. He has since been impossible to trace. It is frustrating that Kitty Vivian volunteered such little knowledge about her aunts even initially denying knowledge of them until prompted. Yet Olive had accompanied the Vivian family, as nanny to Kitty, to France at a time when Kitty was 10 to 12 years old. She must have had some bonding with her aunt, who was a schoolteacher. Kitty was 12 years old when her grandmother died and 13 years old when her grandfather died and her father had organised his funeral. The author understands how some selective amnesia could be produced by the trauma of the Old Bailey trial but, sadly, it has led to simply increasing the shadows around Vivian.

Elizabeth Rosamond, under her adopted form of the name as Rosamund Elizabeth Vincent-Clarke, had asked that no reference to her real age be published. She gave £200 to Olive 'and I wish my executor to pay it to her as soon as possible after my decease'. The rest of her money, £688 with her furniture, was to be divided equally between her children, but she especially left her portrait to her son 'Alan' who was to be her executor.

It was in 1939 that Vivian's own daughter was married. Having spent her formative education at the girl's boarding school of Crofton Grange, Orpington as a boarder, Kitty Vivian went off to France where she spent some time. She was fluent in French and later went for a course at the Sorbonne, the premier university of Paris.[16] On her return to London, in the days just before the Second World War, she was working at the Belgian Embassy.

She had met Anthony Southcliffe Ashton, a year older than she, the son of Thomas Southcliffe Ashton (1889–1968) who was then Dean of the Faculty of Economics at Manchester, and a well-known historian and author of a major study on the Industrial Revolution. He later became Emeritus Professor of Economic History at London University [*The Times*, September 24 1968]. His mother was Mrs

Marion Hague Ashton. Anthony Ashton had been educated at Manchester Grammar School and Hertford College, Oxford. He was then working as a clerk in the Government's Overseas Trade Department. With war looming, he had enlisted in the reserve as a Private (7599477) in the 3rd London Ordnance Field Regiment. They were married on October 28, 1939, at Kensington Register Office. By the end of the war he had achieved the rank of Lt. Colonel of the RASC.

Kitty stayed at her parent's flat during most of the time Ashton was away on war service. Their first daughter, Theresa (Tess), was born in 1943 and the second, Vivien, in 1948. After the war, Ashton became assistant finance editor on the then *Manchester Guardian*. He went on to fulfil various business appointments such as financial director of the Posts and Telecommunications Board and then of the Provincial Insurance Company, retiring in 1974. But even in retirement, Anthony Ashton took on various appointments, such as director of the Oxford University Business Summer School, Trustee of the Post Office Pension Fund, and vice-president of the Hertford College Society.

Kitty became interested in Georgian literature and published various translations from French and Georgian under the name Katharine Vivian for the Folio Society and Octagon Press.[17] Anthony Ashton, her husband, died in 2006, and she died in 2010 on August 12, in Highgate Nursing Home, London (*The Times*, August 17, 2010).

The major disaster for any potential biographer of Vivian's work occurred in 1941. 'An incendiary bomb damaged our flat,' recalled Kitty.[18] 'I cannot give you much help, as most of our family papers were destroyed, as were [Vivian's] agent, John Farquharson.'[19] She recalled: 'Again, our flat in Longridge Road was hit by an incendiary bomb, which damaged only the upper part. I was away at the time, and as far as I remember my parents were not in the flat. Most of our things were destroyed in the warehouse to which we sent them, I forgot when. My parents stayed at a hotel in Bayswater until they moved into the flat in Bramham Gardens. There was no drama in any of this, only inconvenience. The date was sometime in 1941.'[20]

The date was, in fact, the evening of Saturday, May 10 1941, when London suffered its most damaging attack of the year. The Luftwaffe flew 541 sorties over the city, killing more than 1,400 civilians, destroying 5,000 private houses and making 12,000 people homeless, some of them for the second or third time. The glows of the fires lit the London skyline for three entire days. But this raid was, in fact, the final raid of the Blitz, although bombing raids continued until the end of the war. The Luftwaffe never again massed over the skies of British cities in such force. However, the night of May 10 1941 left many houses in Longbridge Road as charred ruins.[21] It was a difficult time with Marion engaged as an Air Raid Warden while Vivian was doing his bit with spells of fire-watching.

This destruction irrevocably closed many doors on any paths to clarifying and clearing up the numerous mysteries of the life of E. Charles Vivian.

As can be expected of a writer of Vivian's calibre, he used the incident to dramatic effect in *Other Gods* (1945). His character Rosalind has refused to leave London during the Blitz.

'She was not frightened—at least, not badly frightened, except when the house was shaken by near-by bombs. One house opposite the end of Mallinson Place had been totally destroyed, with some few people killed. Earl's Court and the west end of Cromwell Road seemed to be getting it badly. Onslow Square had been knocked about, but the people who had talked about all London being destroyed by German bombs were fools ... and, in the jargon of the time, London could take it, and so could Rosalind.[22]

Stanton, her husband, returns to London the day after the massive raid on the City of London, on October 29/30. He tries to persuade Rosalind to leave. 'The widely separated last raids of the Blitz on London came ... ' Rosalind had been out dancing at the Cafe des Folies. The place had been caught in the raid and Rosalind had been killed.

Nothing, of course, quite so dramatic happened to Vivian and his wife. Nevertheless, even after May 10, and the destruction of their home, Vivian and Marion did not contemplate moving out of

The Last Years

London. After a while in the hotel in Bayswater, they move into 29 Bramham Gardens, SW5, where Vivian was to spend the rest of his life.

Kitty recalls that it was about the time of the move into Bramham Gardens that her father had a disagreement with his publisher, Ward Lock. She does not know any details except that 'I remember that he felt that Ward Lock had given him a poor deal, while he always spoke well of Wright and Brown and of Robert Hale.[23] But was this really the reason why Vivian departed from Ward Lock? Six months before Vivian's own home had been destroyed, Ward Lock had suffered in two air raids which had destroyed their records and their entire business premises.

On the night of December 27/28, 1940. Warwick House, in Paternoster Row, Ward Lock's headquarters, had been hit by two explosive bombs. Then, two days later, in the same raid that destroyed Wright and Brown's Farringdon Avenue headquarters, Ward Lock's offices and warehouse received a number of direct hits by incendiaries. The publishers were destroyed. 'The firm lost a vast stock of books of every description, its entire collection of file copies of its publications issued during its career of eighty-six years, and thousands of valuable original drawings.'[24]

This raid was the climax of the Luftwaffe's winter blitz, and it was London's most disastrous fire since the Great Fire of 1666. The Luftwaffe had planned the raids for Sunday evening, December 29, for two principal reasons: namely, the absence of many City of London firewatchers, and the abnormally low tide reached by the Thames during the period of attack. Some 130 aircraft loaded exclusively with incendiary bombs caused six huge conflagrations and sixteen major fires. At one time St Paul's Cathedral was ringed by fire and in danger of being overwhelmed. As it was, eight of Wren's priceless churches perished. The whole area, from St Paul's to the Guildhall, was a mass of flames.

Two hundred fire appliances tried to deal with the fires. Fore Street had to be abandoned, and the half-square mile bordered by Moorgate, Aldersgate, Old Street, and Cannon Street became an inferno.

At 20:30 hours, the Guildhall itself caught alight and the water supply failed. Soon the roof fell in. Engineers had to be called in to blow up areas of buildings to provide firebreaks.

Thankfully for the people of London, at 22:00 hours the weather had started to deteriorate in Northern France and the aircraft of Generalfeldmarschall Albert Kesselring, commanding Luftflotte 2, who had planned the attack to last continuously for nine hours, had to call off his aircraft after only three hours.[25]

The Publishers' Association estimated that more than twenty million volumes held in stock by publishers in the City area had been reduced to charred ruins. For a while, Ward Lock was out of business, without even an address, until Lever Brothers and Unilever made a generous gesture of offering them temporary accommodation in Unilever House on the Embankment. They managed to move to Salisbury Square House, were bombed out once more, and by the end of the war were operating out of St. Bride's Institute, off Fleet Street. These experiences doubtless had an effect on the elderly Lock brothers, trying to run the business with a war-depleted staff. At the end of 1943 Wilfred Lock, the chairman, had to resign from illness caused by the strain and died in October 1945. Leslie Lock took charge and remained chairman until his death in November 1952.[26] Could this have been a contributing factor behind Vivian's change of publishers?

Vivian switched to the publishers Robert Hale in 1942, the same year that Ward Lock published the last of his book written under his 'Barry Lynd' pseudonym.

The fact that Ward Lock was still publishing Vivian's work after the bombing of their headquarters in Warwick House raises another possibility as to why Vivian quit the company. From the time he had joined the firm, his editor had been Douglas Lock, Junior. It was, significantly, in 1942 that Douglas was injured in an air raid and forced to retire. It could well be that the new editor was not as supportive of Vivian's work as Douglas Lock had been.[27]

The 'Barry Lynd' westerns were undoubtedly the weakest of Vivian's output. They were strictly genre formula writing, aimed at a library audience who would pick up a western just because it was a western. Vivian had been persuaded into that western genre, doubtlessly purely for financial inducements, at the end of 1937. His first novel *Trailed Down*, whereby he resurrected his old *Adventure-Story* pseudonym (originally Sydney Barrie Lynd which he had shortened to Barrie Lynd by 1925) appeared from Ward Lock & Co in January 1938.

The books sold at 3s.6d, but were never reissued. In all they numbered six volumes. After *Trailed Down* came *Dude Ranch* (August 1938); *Ghost Canyon* (January 1939); *Riders to Bald Butte* (July 1939); *The Ten Buck Trail* (September 1941) and *George on the Trail* (September 1942).

The Barry Lynd stories followed a set pattern. Usually a stranger rides into town at the start. The storylines were fairly well plotted and were basically murder mysteries with a western setting. Perhaps if Vivian had not attempted to write 'western dialogue' then they might have stood up better. Western dialect writing was obviously not Vivian's forte. Take this passage from *Riders to Bald Butte* as a typical example:

'"That air town is bad, plumb bad," Si averred. "Okeeche County don't want it, and thishyer Franklin's County which is whar we is don't want it. Up to ten year back, the year Millie hyar went to college, thar warn't no doubt it b'longed in Okeeche, but then the big flood shifted Timson's Creek to run west o' the town, which before then it run east, an' sence then Okeeche argues the creek is the boundary, an' Franklin allows the old creek bed is the dividin line."'[28]

This dialogue makes the six Lynd westerns heavy reading.

It is clear from Vivian's work that he was very interested in American dialects. He had a good ear for his native Norfolk dialect which he uses to good effect in many of his books. In other books he shows that he has gone to considerable pains to research the dialect he uses. For example, in an author's note in *Her Ways Are Death* (1941), Vivian is eloquent on the subject of Dorset dialect.

'I am largely indebted, and also grateful, to Mr A.C. Cox, one of the Hardy players, for the assistance he has so kindly given me over the use of Dorset dialect. I may add that I have not tried to render that dialect either in purity of form that one finds in William Barnes' work, or to pervert it quite to the "bus-and-cinema" monstrosity that has grown out of attempts at combining gangster slang and Hollywood wisecracks with the original Dorset idiom. Rather have I tried to steer a mean course between the two, with the very kind help of Mr Cox's monograph on the subject, and also with the realisation that it is virtually impossible to render dialect by means of attempted phonetic spelling. For instance, Barnes' "hwoam" and "sheades" would convey entirely different sounds to two different readers of his work; bearing this in mind, I have tried to give "Dorset" as I have heard and know it.

'And, Dorset readers will probably tell me, have failed. I shall not love them or their county any the less for it, but will remind any caviller that there is a vast difference between the dialect round Blandford and behind Bridport, and on the eastern and western fringes of the country. The nuances are fine, but perceptible, between village and village, even. Dorset men—and women—bear it as best you can!'[29]

Between 1942 and 1952 Robert Hale, Vivian's new publisher, published seven titles, two of these *Arrested* (February 1949) and *Vain Escape* (July 1952) were, of course, posthumous publications. Today Robert Hale is regarded as merely a library-based publisher. In the 1940s Hale was then a leading and often *avant garde* publisher. There has been a change of corporate identity in much the same way as Mills and Boon have changed their image. Today they are regarded as the premier publisher of 'pulp' romances. In the early decades of this century they were a leading publisher of serious literature. Their authors ranged from Jack London, Frank Gostling, Robert Lynd, Robert Herrick, Gaston Leroux to Mrs Alfred Sidgwick, Hugh Walpole, P.G. Wodehouse, H. de Vere Stacpoole, Eden Phillpotts and William Le Queux.

In the novels Vivian wrote for Robert Hale might lay the answer, or even part of the same answer, to Vivian's departure from Ward

Lock. Most of these stories were a return to the more 'serious novel' rather than detective mysteries. In fact, the first book Robert Hale published, *Curses Come Home*, was a rewritten version of his early novel *Following Feet* (1911). Although Vivian now introduced Inspector Terence Byrne into the pages, it was clearly not a murder mystery. The *Times Literary Supplement* rebuked him for breaking away from the detective mystery format[30] which stung Vivian into writing an uncharacteristic reply to the publication, pointing out it was a novel not a mystery tale.[31] One might speculate that Vivian had taken the manuscript of *Curses Come Home* to Ward Lock and it had been firmly rejected. Ward Lock had already turned down his last 'Charles Cannell' effort in 1932.

Perhaps in annoyance, Vivian looked around for a new publisher and found Robert Hale. *Dangerous Guide* followed in 1943. The third novel produced by Robert Hale, *Samson* (November 1943), was another strange novel, starting off as the serious study of a love tangle but abruptly leaping, in the last third of the book, into a spy thriller. Certainly it was an unusual spy thriller, but a spy thriller nevertheless.

She Who Will Not (August 1945) moved back into the area with which Vivian's readers were more comfortable. It is an excellent murder mystery, but with Inspector Terence Byrne playing second fiddle to Stuart Langton who wins the love of the heroine Stephanie, the daughter of Stephen Cameron Fosdyke, first Baron Eastham.

Oddly enough, the last novel to be published during Vivian's life was *Other Gods* (November 1945) which returns back to Vivian's roots in Norfolk and in which Vivian shows he still has an ear for Norfolk dialect. He even introduces a wilful character named Rosalind who has echoes of the character 'Beth' in *Ash*. There is a moving deathbed scene with his protagonist's mother, Mrs Stanton, which makes one wonder whether Vivian is talking about his own mother's death. As she is dying the old lady calls out 'Henry! Henry come back!' But Stanton's father, estranged from the mother, is named Lionel.

'That last agonised cry of hers—who was "Henry"?—He did not

know. He would never know, he felt—and it was better that he should not know. She had gone after other gods.'

Could Vivian's mother, on her deathbed, have called out the name of her first husband James Whisker? Or, indeed, could the 'Henry' she wanted to come back be the young Charles *Henry* Cannell, who had run away to become Vivian?

Once more this is a powerful novel, with abortion, death and sadness permeating its pages. It is certainly not a piece of genre fiction.

When Vivian died, he left two manuscripts behind. One was published in 1949 and the other in 1952, which seems extraordinary lengthy periods after his death. Were they tucked away at Vivian's home and only discovered later, or were they held up in his agent's or publishers'? Again, we shall never know. According to Kitty Vivian: 'As for *Arrested*, I am fairly sure that it was published, or anyway accepted for publication, during his lifetime. I never heard of *Vain Escape*.'

Arrested (February 1949), by its title, leads one to believe it is a detective thriller. But it is not a police arrest that Vivian has in mind. It is another 'serious novel' concerning human relationships. There is not merely an eternal triangle in the story but an eternal quartet. Eve Perceval has married Ronald Hollis just to get rid of her father's name. Once more the father is a problem, laying his sins on his children. In this case the father has been concerned in drugs trafficking and a murder to cover it up. As she rejects her father, Eve (is this the alter ego of 'Evelyn' Cannell rejecting James Henry back in 1900?) tells him that his actions have ruined the life of her mother and herself—'we are all arrested, stopped dead'.

After marrying Hollis, life is tolerable but she does not love him. In Portugal, pursuing his business affairs, Hollis meets Maria Aquita, the wife of a business investor there. He has a tempestuous affair. Senhor Aquita finds out and challenges him to a duel but Hollis knocks him down and returns to England. He then learns that Maria is about to have his child. Hollis wants to keep his marriage to Eve intact but determines to visit Portugal frequently.

Meanwhile, an unhappy Eve, not knowing of the affair, visits friends on the Welsh border and meets Pietro Vesci, an opera singer, who turns out to be 'Peter West'. They fall in love. There are uncomfortable stirrings of the shadowy 'Daisy West' here.

One day, Hollis leaves the London flat to walk to his office. Aquita is waiting outside and shoots him twice. The reason comes out during Aquita's trial for murder, Aquita is sentenced to death, Maria is left in Valladolid with Hollis's child, and Eve is left looking forward to the return of Peter West from an American tour.

Neither with *Arrested* nor *Vain Escape,* published in July 1952, was there anything to indicate that the author was dead, or that *Vain Escape* was his last novel. Certainly the last chapter is set in June 1944, and from that it appears that Vivian wrote it during the last year of the war. It is a return to the tried and trusted Vivian detective mystery mould, with Inspector Terence Byrne in charge.

When old Francis Sylvester is arrested and charged with the murder of Peter Jordan, a moneylender and blackmailer, every shred of evidence is stacked against him. Sir Herbert Eustace KC, who has appeared in the Inspector Head novel *With Intent to Kill,* feels convinced that Sylvester is incapable of the crime and undertakes his defence. The verdict simply amounts to a 'not proven' acquittal and Sylvester's reputation is still tarnished. John Eustace, son of Sir Herbert, now enters the story, determined to clear Sylvester's name and claim the hand of his niece. Once more we find Vivian's old theme of how children must suffer the sins of their fathers. The blurb says: 'Concerned as much with the study of character as with the ordinary murder mystery, E. Charles Vivian has produced in this book a story which will hold the reader from first to last.' It is certainly one of his more interesting murder mysteries.

It was on May 21, 1947, that Vivian was taken into the Princess Beatrice Hospital. He was suffering from uremia and carcinoma of the prostate from which he died. He was only 64 years old. He was buried on May 27 in a private grave at Brompton Cemetery, off the Fulham Road, SW10.[32] The name that he was buried with was 'Charles Henry Vivian', which appears on his death certificate. In his will he left the sum of £507.10s. Only the *Daily Telegraph* noticed his passing in its obituary column.[33] It was very short notice which stated that he was 'Author of mystery and detective stories, including *Infamous Fame, Ladies in the Case,* and *Jewels Go Back.* (He) Also wrote a *History of Aeronautics*'. It seemed a parsimonious appraisal of his life and work.

Marion, who survived Vivian until 1964, died aged 88 years at 7 Knaresborough Place, Kensington, and was buried in the same grave on November 4, 1964. She left a will of £3,045.

As a study of Vivian's life, the author is aware that this must remain a very unsatisfactory biographical work. Without access to letters, diaries, nor even personal reminiscences, we can only grasp at the shadow and not the substance of the man. Sadly, Kitty Vivian did not feel able to contribute any word sketches or anecdotes about her father which might have put a little more flesh on the skeleton.[34] What becomes obvious is that Vivian, as a person, has been consigned to the shadows. I believe that the reasons for this are obvious. From those facts of his childhood and youth that I have been able to salvage, he consciously tried to draw a veil over his past. He comes across as a rather sad personality who never really came to terms with his unhappy childhood in spite of the many fictional attempts to analyse it. Later in life came the scandal of his affair with Lillian Simmons and the failure of his blackmail charge against her in the Central Criminal Court caused his daughter, Kitty, to attempt to drawn a veil over much of his later life, condemning her father as a complete villain of whom the less that was said, the better.

A study of his work demonstrates that he was not a mere scribbler of words, not just a 'hack' or 'penny a-liner', who was willing to turn out genre fiction just for a pay cheque. In his 'lost race' tales, he showed that he had the an ability to equal H. Rider Haggard at his best in style and story content; in his 'Gees' novels, he demonstrated an undoubted talent as a first class writer of supernatural tales; while, with his Inspector Head novels, he displayed an adroitness and dexterity as a master of the detective mystery novel. He is at least deserving of a niche in the Hall of the Literary Valhalla. The quotation he used in *Curses Come Home* might well have been an epitaph:

'... Unlighted the shrine.
The gold and the incense are gone.
The song and the story are silenced...'

Enthusiasts of the weird fantasy and mystery thriller genres have shown that Vivian's 'song and story' are not yet entirely silenced. It is hoped, too, that this biographical contribution might provide a light, however dim, to illuminate his 'unlighted shrine'.

Notes

1. Katharine Vivian Ashton, letter to author, August 28, 1991.
2. Katharine Vivian Ashton, letter to author, November 4, 1990.
3. Katharine Vivian Ashton, letter to author, September 1, 1990.
4. Katharine Vivian Ashton, letter to author, April 20, 1991.
5. Katharine Vivian Ashton, letter to author, November 7, 1991.
6. *Golden Fleece*, May 1939.
7. Katharine Vivian Ashton, letter to author, October 13, 1993.
8. Katharine Vivian Ashton, letter to author, November 23, 1993.
9. Katharine Vivian Ashton, letter to author, January 28, 1994.
10. Katharine Vivian Ashton, letter to author, March 22, 1990.
11. Katharine Vivian Ashton, letter to author, May 18, 1990.
12. Katharine Vivian Ashton, letter to author, March 18, 1994.
13. Katharine Vivian Ashton, letter to author, March 14, 1994.
14. Death certificate, St Catharine's House, London, and Will, Somerset House, London.
15. Katharine Vivian Ashton, letter to author, May 18, 1990.
16. Katharine Vivian Ashton, letter to author, January 28, 1994.
17. Katharine Vivian Ashton, letter to author, April 23, 1990.
18. Katharine Vivian Ashton, letter to author, November 4, 1990.
19. Katharine Vivian Ashton, letter to author, August 28, 1991.

[20.] Katharine Vivian Ashton, letter to author, October 12, 1991.
[21.] *Kensington News*, May 16, 1941, and *Kensington Post*, May 15, 1941.
[22.] *Other Gods*, Robert Hale, 1945, pp. 311-312.
[23.] Katharine Vivian Ashton, letter to author, November 23, 1993.
[24.] *Adventure in Publishing: The House of Ward Lock 1854-1954*, Edward Liveing, Ward Lock & Co Ltd, London, 1954. pp. 98/99.
[25.] *Battle Over Britain*, Francis K. Mason, 92nd revised ed. Aston Publications Ltd., Bucks., 1990, pp. 389/391.
[26.] *Adventures in Publishing* (above).
[27.] *Ibid.*
[28.] *Riders to the Bald Butte*, Barry Lynd, Ward Lock, 1939, p. 12.
[29.] *Her Ways Are Death*, Jack Mann, Wright and Brown, 1941, see 'Note by Author', p. vi.
[30.] *Times Literary Supplement*, May 23, 1942.
[31.] *Times Literary Supplement*, June 6, 1942.
[32.] No. 19468, Compartment 1W.
[33.] *Daily Telegraph*, May 23, 1947.
[34.] Katharine Vivian Ashton, letter to author, September 24, 1991: 'I am afraid that, although I understand your wish for anecdotes etc., that would involve much more work than I have time for, having work of my own to do.'

E. C. VIVIAN: A SHORT BIBLIOGRAPHY

A chronological checklist of all known editions. Where a pseudonym is used other than E. Charles Vivian, this is indicated.

The Shadow of Christine, Gay & Bird, London, April 1907. US edition: R.F. Fenno, New York, April 1910. (as Evelyn C. H. Vivian).

The Woman Tempted Me, Andrew Melrose, London, September 1909. Reprint: May 1912.

Wandering of Desire, Andrew Melrose, London, September 1910.

Following Feet, Andrew Melrose, London, February 1911.

Passion Fruit, William Heinemann, London, March 1912.

Peru, South American Handbook, Pitman, London, July 1914. US edition: D. Appleton, New York, 1914.

The British Army from Within, Hodder and Stoughton, November 1914 (simultaneous cloth 2s.6d. and paper covers 2s. editions) Reprint: December 1915. US edition: George H. Doran, New York, 1914.

Divided Ways, Holden & Hardingham, November 1914.

With the Royal Army Medical Corps at the Front, *Daily Telegraph* War Book, Hodder and Stoughton, 1914.

With the Scottish Regiments at the Front, *Daily Telegraph* War Book, Hodder and Stoughton, 1914 (this title was not actually published until January 1915).

The Way of the Red Cross, co-author J.E. Hodder-Williams, Preface Queen Alexandra, for *The Times*, Hodder and Stoughton, London, July 1915. US edition: George H. Doran, New York, 1915.

The Young Man Absalom, Chapman and Hall, London, January 1915. US edition: E. P. Dutton, New York, July 1915.

A History of Aeronautics, William Collins, London, May 1921. US edition: Harcourt, 1921.

The Yellow Streak, Warwick Bros & Rutter, Toronto, 1921.

City of Wonder, Hutchinson, London, January 1923. Reprint: *Adventure-Story* Library edition: February 1924. Serial: *Adventure-Story* September 1922—December 1922. US edition: Moffatt, 1923. US magazine: *Famous Fantastic Mysteries*, October 1947. US edition: 'Time-Lost Series', Centaur Press, New York, paperback, $1.25. November 1973.

A Scout of the '45, Boys Own Paper, London, October 1923. Reprint, May 1930.

The Guarded Woman, Charles Cannell, Hutchinson, London, April 1923.

Fields of Sleep, Hutchinson, London, July 1923. Reprint: January 1925. Serial: *Adventure-Story*, May 1923—April 1923. US: as *Valley of Silent Men*, *Famous Fantastic Mysteries*, August 1949. US edition: Donald M. Grant Inc., 1980.

Broken Couplings, Charles Cannell, Hutchinson, London, August 1923. Reprint: January 1927.

People of Darkness, Hutchinson, London, April 1924. Reprint: August 1925. Serial: *Adventure-Story*, February 1924—May 1924.

Barkery's Drift, Charles Cannell, Hutchinson, London, April 1924. Reprint: March 1926. reprint: Ward Lock edition with Vivian's by-line, 1936.

Ash, Charles Cannell, Hutchinson, London, January 1925. Reprint: March 1926.

Star Dust, Hutchinson, London, March 1925.

The Guardian of the Cup, Charles Cannell, Hodder and Stoughton, London, 1925. Reprint: Ward Lock edition as by Vivian, 1935 (see No 58).

The Lady of the Terraces, Hodder and Stoughton, London, December 1925.

A King There Was, Hodder and Stoughton, London, May 1926.

E. C. Vivian: A Short Bibliography

The Passionless Quest, Charles Cannell, Hodder & Stoughton, June 1926.

The Forbidden Door, Ward Lock, London, September 1927. Reprint: May 1928; March 1929; January 1931.

Robin Hood and His Merry Men, Sunshine Series, Ward Lock, London, September 1927. Reprint: September 1933; October 1934; August 1935; September 1950; October 1950.

Man Alone, Ward Lock, London, January 1928. Reprint: January 1929; January 1930.

Nine Days, Ward Lock, London, June 1928. Reprint: April 1929; February 1931; September 1933.

The Moon and Chelsea, Charles Cannell, Ward Lock, London, September 1928. Reprint: July 1929; November 1931.

Shooting Stars adapted from Anthony Asquith's screenplay, Hurst and Blackett, London, October 1928.

The Tale of Fleur, Ward Lock, London, February 1929. Reprint: October 1931.

Woman Dominant, Ward Lock, London, July 1929. Reprint: April 1930; February 1932.

Double or Quit, Ward Lock, London, January 1930. Reprint: June 1932.

One Tropic Night, Ward Lock, London, May 1930. Reprint April 1930.

Delicate Fiend, Ward Lock, London, May 1930. Reprint: November 1931; June 1932.

Unwashed Gods, Ward Lock, London, January 1931. Reprint: February 1931; August 1933.

Innocent Guilt, Ward Lock, London, July 1931. Reprint: April 1932 and in 1934.

And the Devil, Charles Cannell, John Lane, The Bodley Head, London, November 1931. Reprint: March 1933.

Infamous Fame, Ward Lock, London, January 1932. Reprint: January 1933; January 1935.

Lone Isle, Ward Lock, London, May 1932. Reprint: May 1935.

False Truth, Ward Lock, London, September 1932. Reprint: July 1933; September 1935.

Reckless Coulson, Jack Mann, Wright and Brown, London, January 1933.

The Keys of the Flat, Ward Lock, London, January 1933. Reprint: November 1933; June 1936.

The Ladies in the Case, Ward Lock, London, April 1933. Reprint: August 1937.

Girl in the Dark, Ward Lock, London, April 1933. Reprint: July 1934; July 1937. US edition: T.V. Boardman & Co, New York, 1942.

Coulson Goes South, Jack Mann, Wright and Brown, London, September 1933. Reprint: August 1934; August 1938.

Shadow on the House, Ward Lock, London, January 1934. Reprint: July 1935; June 1938.

The Dead Man's Chest, Jack Mann, Wright and Brown, London, January 1934. Reprint: February 1935; November 1939. US edition: Godwin, New York, 1934.

Egyptian Nights, Jack Mann, Wright and Brown, London, January 1934.

Jewels Go Back, Ward Lock, London, April 1934. Reprint: February 1937.

Accessory After, Ward Lock, London, April 1934. Reprint: November 1935; February 1939.

House for Sale, Amalgamated Press (*Thriller* Library No 12), London, 1934 [rewritten as *With Intent to Kill*, No 65].

Seventeen Cards, Ward Lock, London, January 1935. Reprint: January 1936; January 1937; July 1939.

The Guardian of the Cup, Ward Lock, March 1935 (originally issued as by Charles Cannell).

Detective Coulson, Jack Mann, Wright and Brown, London, June 1935. Reprint: June 1936; November 1936. Canadian edition: Ryerson Press, Toronto.

The Capsule Mystery, Ward Lock, London, June 1935. Reprint: September 1938.

Cigar for Inspector Head, Ward Lock, London, September 1935. Reprint: April 1936; April 1937; January 1940.

Who Killed Gatton, Ward Lock, London, January 1936. Reprint: January 1937; August 1940.

Barker's Drift, Ward Lock, February 1936 (originally issued as by Charles Cannell).

Coulson Alone, Jack Mann, Wright and Brown, London, April 1936. Reprint: April 1937; April 1939.

With Intent To Kill, Ward Lock, London, July 1936. Reprint: April 1937; June 1940.

The Black Prince, Ward Lock (Sentinel Series), London, August 1936.

Gee's First Case, Jack Mann, Wright & Brown, October 1936. Reprint: September 1937. US edition: Bookfinger, New York, 1970.

Tramp's Evidence, Ward Lock, London, January 1937. Reprint: January 1938. US edition: as *Barking Dog Mystery*, Clue Club Mystery series, Hillman Curl, New York, 1937. US edition: as *Barking Dog Mystery*, McLeod (90 cent paperback).

Grey Shapes, Jack Mann, Wright and Brown, London, March 1937. Reprint: February 1938. US edition: Bookfinger, New York, 1970.

.38 Automatic, Ward Lock, London, August 1937. Reprint: January 1939.

Nightmare Farm, Jack Mann, Wright and Brown, London, September 1937. Reprint: September 1938. US edition: Bookfinger, New York, 1975.

Evidence in Blue, Ward Lock, London, January 1938. Reprint: January 1939. US edition: as *Man in Gray*. Clue Club Mystery edition, Hillman Curl, New York, 1938. US edition: *Man in Gray*, MacLeod, 90 cent paperback, 1938.

Trailed Down, Barry Lynd, Ward Lock, London, January 1938.

The Kleinert Case, Jack Mann, Wright and Brown, February 1938. Reprint: March 1939.

Dude Ranch, Barry Lynd, Ward Lock, London, August 1938.

The Rainbow Puzzle, Ward Lock, London, September 1938. Reprint: April 1939.

Maker of Shadows, Jack Mann, Wright and Brown, London, November 1938. Reprint: October 1939. US Serial: *Argosy*, December 9, 1939— January 6, 1940. US edition: Bookfinger, 1977.

Problem by Rail, Ward Lock, London, January 1939. Reprint: January 1940.

Ghost Canyon, Barry Lynd, Ward Lock, London, January 1939.

The Ninth Life, Jack Mann, Wright and Brown, London, June 1939. Reprint: June 1940. US Serial: *Argosy*. August 5, 1939—August 26, 1939. US Magazine: *Merritt's Fantasy Magazine*, April 1950. US edition: Bookfinger, New York, 1970.

Riders to Bald Butte, Barry Lynd, Ward Lock, London, July 1939.

Touch and Go, Ward Lock, London, September 1939. Reprint: May 1940.

The Impossible Crime, Ward Lock, London, January 1940.

The Glass Too Many, Jack Mann, Wright and Brown, London, July 1940. US edition: Bookfinger, New York, 1973.

Man with a Scar, Ward Lock, London, September 1940.

And Then There Was One, Ward Lock, March 1941. Reprint: February 1942.

Her Ways Are Death, Jack Mann, Wright and Brown, London, 1941 [originally intended for Spring, 1941, issue. First edition was caught in bombing of publishers, surviving copies were then put out in a reprint jacket]. US Magazine: *Famous Fantastic Mysteries*, June 1952. US edition: Bookfinger, New York, 1981.

The Ten Buck Trail, Barry Lynd, Ward Lock, London, November 1941.

Curses Come Home, Robert Hale, London, May 1942.

George on the Trail, Barry Lynd, Ward Lock, London, September 1942.

Dangerous Guide, Robert Hale, London, June 1943.

Samson, Robert Hale, November 1944. Canadian edition: Ryerson, Toronto.

She Who Will Not, Robert Hale, London, August 1945.

Other Gods, Robert Hale, London, November 1945.

Arrested, Robert Hale, February 1949.

Vain Escape, Robert Hale, July 1952.

Acknowledgments

In chasing 'The Shadow of Mr Vivian' over many years, a great many people contributed to my researches. I should like to make a special acknowledgment to the late Mrs Katharine Vivian Ashton (1917–2010), the daughter of E. Charles Vivian, for all the information and material that she sent me over a period of nearly five years and to her daughter, Mrs Tess Blondel.

I would like to express my sincerest gratitude to my researcher at the time, Elizabeth Murray, and to my fellow 'literary morticians'— Jack Adrian; in particular to Mike Ashley; to Richard Dalby, and the late Peter Haining (1940–2007)—without whose help, advice, and enthusiasm this project would never have been brought to a completion. I am aware that since I started my researches at the request of Donald M. Gant in the late 1970s, many, who have help supply information, have 'shuffled off this mortal coil'. I beg forgiveness of their Shades if I have missed or overlooked the dates of their departure from this 'Vale of Tears'.

Thanks are also due to Dr Ruth Hadman of Bedingham and to members of the Cannell family: Frank G. Cannell, David Cannell, Miss A. M. Walton MBE, Joyce Bond, and R.S. Bennett. Also to Ben Burgess MBE.

To Major Jim Etherington, Regimental Secretary of The Royal Dragoons, and his colleague Captain C. Boardman; to Angela Kelsall of the National Army Museum; to Ion Trewin (formerly of Hodder and Stoughton); to Mrs Jean Rose ALA, deputy group librarian of the Octopus Publishing Group Library; to Phil Wickham of the British Film Institute; to Dennis Northmore of Brooklyn; to Caroline Belgrave of Curtis Brown and John Farquharson Ltd; to Ann Beresford, Elizabeth Beresford (1926–2010), and Marcus Beresford aka Mark Brandel (1919–1994); to Jon Wynne-Tyson; and to late Tessa Sayle (1931–1993) who was Vivian's agent and The Sayle Literary Agency.

Thanks are also due to the staffs of the British Library together with the Colindale Newspaper Library, the Public Record Office, Bodleian Library, Oxford, St Catharine's House, and Somerset House, London.

To David Robert Wooten of Charleston, South Carolina, who saved my original typescript from oblivion.

Last, but in no way least, my thanks to the late Don Grant of Donald M. Grant Publisher Ltd, Rhode Island, USA, who wrote me a letter on October 22, 1976, asking if I knew anything about the life of E. Charles Vivian. This is a rather belated, full reply to the question!

Peter Berresford Ellis, historian, biographer and novelist, has published critically acclaimed biographies of H. Rider Haggard, Captain W. E. Johns and Talbot Mundy. Under his pseudonym, Peter Tremayne, he is best known for his award winning, international bestselling historical crime series—The Sister Fidelma Mysteries. They have appeared in eighteen languages. *The Guardian* once claimed Sister Fidelma to be among the top ten fictional nuns in literature.

Born in Coventry and educated in Brighton and London, his degrees are in Celtic Studies and he has been acknowledged as one of the foremost authorities on Celtic history and culture. In spite of this specialisation, he has always been interested in popular literature, reviewing and also writing biographical sketches of writers for a wide variety of newspapers and journals as well as producing his own fictional works.

Considered a prolific writer, he published nearly one hundred titles under his own name and his pseudonym as well as a similar number of short stories as Peter Tremayne.